FOR A NEW AFRICA
With Hope and Dignity

The visit which this book records became a reality through the collaboration of several programmes of the WCC: the Africa Desk, the International Affairs team, and the multicultural ministry programme of the Mission and Ecumenical Formation Team.

We would like to thank the All Africa Conference of Churches, the National Council of Churches of Kenya and the Protestant Council of Rwanda for their key roles in ensuring that the visit and the workshop on "Lasting Peace in Africa" were a success. We are also grateful to those who made additional contributions, especially the WCC's moderator His Holiness Aram I who, in spite of not being able to be present in person, provided his papers to be part of this record.

Our thanks go also to Nicholas Otieno who worked on the documentation and the text for this publication.

REV. DR ANDRÉ KARAMAGA
WCC AFRICA DESK

Cover and design: CLAUDE-DOMINIQUE BÉGUIN

ISBN 2-8254-1413-1

© 2004 WCC Publications
World Council of Churches
P.O.Box 2100
150 route de Ferney
1211 GENEVA 2
Switzerland
Website: http://www.wcc-coe.org

Printed in France

FOR A NEW
AFRICA
With Hope and Dignity

TABLE OF CONTENTS

1

PREFACE

More than seven hundred years ago, Africa was a land of unimaginable wealth, to the mythical proportions of King Solomon's mines. It was a land blessed not only with ivory, myrrh and spices but also with institutions of wisdom such as the well-respected academy of Timbuktu, which became a global centre of research and scholarship in mathematics, astronomy, the creative arts and theology. The moral wealth and scientific ingenuity of the continent were so awesome that they inspired a vision of life typified in the construction of the mysterious Nubian pyramids in Egypt.

God still provides enough to supply every human need in the variety of African resources, including the flora and fauna of every type and kind in this wonderful continent. Precious metals, minerals, oil of unbelievable abundance, the largest and deepest rivers and lakes on earth such as the Nile, the Congo, the Niger, Victoria meander to the deep oceans surrounding the continent. The great voyages of Westerners to the east scouted through the African hinterland leaving traces of encounters of cultures and peoples from all parts of the world. All these are the exquisite evidence that God, indeed, loves Africa!

African churches place a high priority on their schools.

But why has Africa been swallowed by negative forces of history, eroding her dignity and self-respect as the mother of all humankind? Why does she beg for emergency food aid today and seek cheap drugs and vaccines for the health of her people through tough loans that she receives under the most demeaning conditions? What is the origin of the state of impoverishment and hopelessness that breeds the widening restlessness and conflict in this beautiful continent?

Given the atrocious impact of the African slave trade, abolished only towards the end of the 19th century, the enduring colonial project and the alienating power of globalization, the 21st century offers the opportunity of a new African century. This is an opportunity not only for recovery but also of renaissance in which the continent will re-awaken from an age dominated by hegemonic forces of occupation to a new era of dignity and freedom!

It is therefore imperative, by virtue of the burden of history and her moral heritage, that the struggles of Africa be focused on reinventing her identity apart from the constraints of colonial memory in order to embrace God's will, not only for her sake but also for the future of humanity. In so doing, Africa has the ethical responsibility to face her own reality and gather new strength through an ethical and spiritual process of healing. That is why, on behalf of the global ecumenical family, the World Council of Churches is paying special homage to Africa in order to share the vision of hope for a new world in which poverty, injustice, tyranny, war and genocide will never again reign. The definitive moment for Africa is at hand, and it is for this reason that the WCC has given a special place to Africa. Through various programmatic initiatives, the council has been instrumental in accompanying the churches and people of God of Africa while proclaiming God's intention for the continent, "Behold, I create a new Africa!"

Songs of praise animate African worship and contribute to the rhythm of life.

The visit to Kenya and Rwanda in April 2004 by the leadership of the World Council of Churches and the All Africa Conference of Churches is a clear indication of the commitment of the global and continental ecumenical family to accompany local churches as they work with other civil society institutions in proclaiming the dawn of a new Africa. The World Council of Churches (WCC) is the world's broadest and most inclusive ecumenical fellowship of churches, an organization which enjoys a membership of more than 340 churches from virtually all Christian traditions in 120 countries on all continents. The Roman Catholic Church works cooperatively with the WCC although it is not a member of the WCC.

The moderator of the WCC, His Holiness Catholicos Aram I, was to have made a pastoral visit to Kenya and Rwanda in April 2004, together with the WCC's general secretary, the Rev. Dr Samuel Kobia. In the end, the moderator was unable to make this visit, so Dr Kobia led the delegation on behalf of His Holiness. Two presentations prepared by the moderator and shared in Africa are included in this publication.

The moderator presides over the WCC central committee – the highest policy making organ after the WCC assembly which he also chairs. The WCC was formally inaugurated in 1948 in Amsterdam. The council's staff is headed by the general secretary, Dr Samuel Kobia, a Kenyan and the first African to hold the position.

The delegation from the WCC visited Africa at the invitation of the All Africa Conference of Churches (AACC), the National Council of Churches of Kenya (NCCK) and the Protestant Council of Rwanda. The AACC is a fellowship of 169 national churches in 39 African countries enjoying a congregational membership of 120 million Christians. The delegation included, among others, Dr Agnes Abuom, one of the WCC presidents, AACC president the Rt Rev. Nyansako Ni-Nku, AACC general secretary Rev. Dr H. Mvume Dandala, and other members of WCC staff including Mrs Teny Pirri-Simonian, executive secretary for Church and Ecumenical Relations, the Rev. Dr André Karamaga, executive secretary for Africa, and Mr Peter Weiderud, director of the WCC Commission of Churches on International Affairs.

The delegation met with local ecumenical partners, church leaders, congregations and people from all walks of life, as well as the heads of government in both Kenya and Rwanda. In Rwanda, a workshop on lasting peace in Africa was organized to coincide with the visit of the WCC delegation. The content of this booklet is intended to provide institutional memory of the messages of hope delivered at various venues in both countries, a witness that reached its climax at the national stadium in Kigali on April 18th, 2004.

A TESTIMONY FROM THE HEART

I was looking forward with joy to my visit to this blessed land of Kenya and to joining you in praising God for granting this opportunity to Samuel Kobia to serve the ecumenical movement, which I believe is a gift of the Holy Spirit. Due to unforeseen reasons, I cannot be with you. I remember fondly my first visit to Kenya when I attended the fifth assembly of the World Council of Churches as a young delegate of my church in 1975.

I first met Samuel 13 years ago and have seen, in this humble servant of God, a devout Christian and a committed ecumenist. He has conscientiously served the ecumenical movement, in particular the WCC, which is the movement's global and most comprehensive manifestation, during a challenging time in its history. Serving the ecumenical movement is a calling integral to the Christian vocation. I am confident that, with his profound sense of calling, Samuel will give the best of his talents and gifts to the ecumenical movement. As you know, he is the first African general secretary of the council. Therefore, he will certainly bring Africa to the ecumenical movement and take the ecumenical movement to Africa with renewed vision and commitment.

I know the deep concerns, complex problems and great challenges that Africa is facing. The WCC has always been with Africa: against apartheid, racism, injustice and poverty, and supportive of development, nation-building, democratization and programmes to combat HIV/AIDS. An important expression of the council's commitment to Africa came in 1998 after the Harare Assembly, in the form of a new programme: "The Ecumenical Focus on Africa". As the moderator of the central committee of the WCC, I want to assure you that the council will continue to stand with Africa. May God bless this continent and this beautiful country.

Catholicos Aram I and the Rev. Samuel Kobia, of the WCC.

By His Holiness Aram I

3
A NEW DAWN FOR AFRICA

I feel humbled to share my reflections with you on an occasion that reflects God's will for Africa. When the AACC held its last assembly of the 20th century in Addis Ababa, in October 1997, church leaders across the continent who gathered at the assembly resolved prophetically that the 21st century would be a century for Africa. Little did they know then in what form an answer to their prayer would be manifested.

We are now celebrating our Lord's mysterious way of responding to prayers. Through our brother, the Rev. Dr Samuel Kobia, God has given Africa a responsibility to head the church in the world. Who would have imagined, even faintly, that there would come a time for Africa to take the exciting responsibility of providing leadership to the global ecumenical movement at the dawn of this century.

It is one thing to dream dreams, yet it is another to petition God through prayers; the big question however is: to what extent is, or was, Africa ready for this responsibility?

The president of the AACC with the general secretaries of the WCC and AACC.

The Rev. Samuel Kobia's appointment to the substantial position of general secretary of the World Council of Churches is indeed a cause for celebration but also a challenge to Africa as a whole. There are those who will be saying, Let us see if Africans can make it. Given the image of Africa that has always been painted by the world media, there are those who believe that nothing good can come out of Africa. They may even be saying that the selection of the Rev. Samuel Kobia was an unfortunate accident.

BY RT REV.
NYANSAKO NI-NKU

We, however, know too well that God does not make mistakes. We also know that our loving God does not operate accidentally. We know that when the infant Jesus Christ needed a place for refuge during his formative years, it was Africa that God provided 2000 years ago, and that was not by accident. It is also not by accident that Christianity appears 2000 years later to be taking refuge in Africa, so to speak, as it gradually shifts its centre of gravity to Africa. Equally, it is not an accident that God, in the divine plan for history, has for the first time placed an African at the steering wheel of the global ecumenical movement.

We in Africa, therefore, have a duty to give our brother Samuel Kobia all due support. Following his election, we can no longer sit on the periphery of the global stage. God is telling us that it is time we moved to the centre stage of global action through the ecumenical movement.

4

TO GOD BE THE GLORY

I want to pay tribute to you all beginning with my own family which extends from my wife and children to the whole community of the people of God in Kenya and in Africa. You have nourished me with hope and granted me the space to grow and become who I am today. As Christians, as Africans and Kenyans, we are a people of memory. The narrative memory of the life of Jesus which we just celebrated in the feast of the resurrection is what draws us together from a variety of faith traditions to be in communion with one another, because we are all created by the same events that led to the salvation of humankind. In this regard I cannot help but remember the days when we traveled together through the turbulence in the high seas of politics. It was then that I served among you even before I became the general secretary of the National Council of Churches of Kenya.

I worked with the development programmes of the council and learnt many things about serving under the then General Secretary of NCCK, Mr John Kamau, in the mid-eighties. We planted the seeds of hope together for this great nation. And in fact most of us even risked our lives in solidarity with the suffering and the voiceless in our society. I would like to believe that what we did together as churches brought about something to be treasured by future generations of Kenyans.

I am glad of the continuity of this work through my successor, the Rev. Mutava Musyimi. The legacy of ecumenical engagement will continue to flourish and become part of our spiritual and national treasure for generations to come. I recall how seriously we took our prophetic mandate, articulating the imperatives of good governance and the ethical values of participatory democracy in the moral formation of our citizens. It has been a long journey, and the promise lives on.

The Rev. Jesse Kamau with Nkatha Kobia (left) and Kaburo Kobia (right), with the Rev. M. Mutava.

BY THE REV. DR SAMUEL KOBIA

I have since then received my calling again to move on to Geneva, but my heart has always been with you and the whole continent of Africa. Our struggles as a church always led us to affirm the dignity and humanity of our people. And when I see young people in our churches singing and working side by side with their pastors, it gives me great joy and hope that tomorrow will never be lost. This has always been the source of my inspiration, that to live a meaningful life and to find joy is to serve others from one's heart. For the real enemies of life are not the ones we lock in prisons, but the real enemy is to be found within the weak dark corners of the soul where the horrors of hatred have reclaimed the pure desire to Love and to be Loved.

To relinquish these fetters of fear and brave our way to the unyielding moment of truth let us extinguish the fire of desire with the insurmountable patience of a new revolution of the heart. The resolve in one's heart to serve God and humankind is the greatest gift of all. Every gift from God comes with responsibility and accountability. And on my own I could never do it because the responsibility I now carry touches not only the ecumenical life of the church worldwide, but it also influences the thinking and orientation concerning our shared responsibility to make this world a safe place for the abundant life of all humankind. So this is truly a great privilege, to stand in the presence of God and renew my commitment to serve the church and the world.

This is truly a humbling moment for me because I know that I am not alone. Let us continue to provide that space in which the churches speak with one voice and affirm the good things that are happening, and caution regarding things that need a remedy. There are times to raise one's voice on the rooftops but there are also times to speak with a gentle voice. As one great poet once said, the greatest thing ever said is that which is spoken without words. I have no more words but a silent embrace of the love that fills this sanctuary today. In the echo of the silent footsteps of a faithful pilgrim on a journey through the valley of pain and despair, we must continue together with the great song that suits every situation, "To God Be the Glory".

This is my prayer: In the absence of all fear, may freedom, justice, peace, and harmony remain lit in the streets and every household of Africa. We at the World Council of Churches will continue to accompany the churches in Kenya, Africa and the world, as we enter the new frontiers of evangelism in the 21st century. And for the sake of Kenya and Africa, let us always remember that if you want to go fast, walk alone; but, if you want to go far, walk with others!

The Hon. Stephen Kalonzo Musyoka at a reception hosted by the Coptic Church.

5
MESSAGE TO THE HEAD OF STATE

Your Excellency, I hereby bring you greetings from the entire fellowship of churches all over the world, united under the leadership of the World Council of Churches in Geneva. We would like to express our solidarity with your government and commend you for the good signs of a new promising future for Kenya. We thank God for the Kenyan people and the democratic gains that bequeathed your leadership with the task of rebuilding this great nation.

Your Excellency, this is my first official pastoral visit since my election as the general secretary of the World Council of Churches. I have come back home to my country to seek the blessings of the people of God in Kenya, as I embark on the task of guiding the ecumenical movement in the new frontiers of our mission in the 21st century. Africa has a very special place in the life and work of the WCC. During our last assembly in Harare, Zimbabwe, we initiated a special focus on Africa together with the All Africa Conference of Churches (AACC) and the national councils of churches in the entire continent. In Kenya we have special collaboration with NCCK in various activities and projects that promote human development.

The WCC, together with a network of Christian communities, civil society agencies and churches worldwide, have continued to work in the areas of education, health and food security. We are engaged in affirming the dignity and life of the poor and transforming the human condition with the vision and values of the gospel. The churches in Kenya, from the missionary movement to date, continue to play a major role in complementing the work of government in all critical areas of human development. We celebrate and encourage their good work and applaud the goodwill and co-operation your government continues to give in this noble endeavour.

Kenyan president Excellency Mwai Kibaki, accompanied by Samuel and Ruth Kobia and the Rev. M. Mutava (left).

By the Rev. Dr Samuel Kobia

As you are aware, your Excellency, the churches have been involved through the work of the WCC in the ongoing peace processes and initiatives in the continent. Our historic contribution goes way back to the struggles against apartheid in South Africa and has continued through the most recent peace initiatives in Liberia and Sudan. We are very encouraged by the exemplary efforts of your government through IGAD to bring lasting peace to the horn of Africa. It is our prayer that the facilitation you have provided in the ongoing peace talks will bear fruit and relieve the pain and suffering of the people of Somalia and Sudan.

Your Excellency, we trust that the relationship between your government and the churches in Kenya will continue to flourish for the good and well-being of the people of Kenya. As church and state we are all called to affirm the human dignity and democratic values of all peoples and, working together, to bring health and wholeness especially to those suffering from HIV/AIDS. We express our gratitude for your personal commitment to the prevention and eradication of this dreadful disease and assure you that through the ecumenical initiative on HIV/AIDS in Africa we shall continue to complement the work of your government. We assure you of our prayers and gratitude to God for sustaining you in good health. May the blessings and peace of our risen Lord embrace you, your government and the people of Kenya for generations to come!

6

AFRICA AND THE ECUMENICAL MOVEMENT

1. INTRODUCTION

*Dr Agnes Abuom,
WCC president
for Africa.*

BY DR AGNES ABUOM

Christianity came into the continent with a burden of European history and as a divided movement with a variety of claims that reflected the conflicts and contradictions of the colonial heritage. Our endeavour to create an ecumenical space in which churches reflect and respond in solidarity with one another and the people of the Africa is critical for the journey of the self-renewal of the Church. We are on the threshold of a new moment in history, and we have the means to redefine who we are and even reclaim our place as Africans beyond that which has been compromised by global forces and hegemonies.

Our hope is anchored in the fact that God has not left Africa alone. So long as our commitment is connected to the transforming power of God in all creation, we shall change the conditions of alienation, anguish and misery of the African people. As the continent and her peoples are constantly in the grip of political and economic despondency, we must remember that our hope is deeply embedded in the resilience and vigilance of the word of God which speaks to us in the spirits of our ancestors, and which was ultimately revealed in the exemplary life and values for which Jesus lived, died and triumphed over death.

Our commitment to a new sustainable future is therefore anchored in the common values of proclaiming the good news beyond hegemonic discourses on development. The centrality and meaning in proclaiming anew the promise of a new future ought to reflect our capacity to be good neighbours to each other. The ecumenical movement in Africa ought to provide the social space of good neighbourhood in which the relationship between peoples and institutions are guided by the gospel promise of abundant life (John 10: 10). Every activity in our institutions must remain structured around solidarity with the weak and the excluded in society.

Africa must arise once again with the renewed confidence to reclaim her place in history and in the modern world. The ecumenical movement is therefore an invaluable social and theological instrument of hope for Africa. Through the programmatic life of ecumenical agencies in the continent we endeavour to provide space for moral replenishment and recovery from contemporary social and political traumas which have led to apathy and loss of confidence in the continent.

Our present challenge is to focus on how to harness our strengths, gather available resources and embark on the new path for the sake of the future of the church in Africa. From the national council of churches, regional fellowships and with the leadership of member churches of the WCC and the AACC together we are called to initiate a process of reinventing the ecumenical movement in Africa.

2. CHALLENGES OF THE ECUMENICAL MOVEMENT

The ecumenical movement must be transformed into an organic space of reflection and dialogue that may serve in enlightening leaders, including policy makers. Institutional expressions of the movement in the continent must then reclaim their place as repositories of living memories in a sanctuary of unity not just for the churches but also the civil society and other instruments of governance which include the nation-state in Africa. There are various examples of such a paradigm that have been actualized historically, for example the conciliar processes that led to the establishment by WCC of the programme to combat racism in South Africa. This certainly helped the world to see the oppression of Africa with new eyes and named apartheid for what it was. The moral and ethical claims of solidarity were not just informed by the human rights regime but by the naming of apartheid as a sin against God and humanity. Nelson Mandela affirmed this theological thinking during his profound message to the World Council of Churches assembly held at Harare in December 1998.

Africa brought a new reality of prophetic engagement within the civic public realm. The diakonia work in solidarity with the liberation movements in Africa from the seventies and eighties

The children of Africa look to a brighter future.

equipped the churches and social movements in solidarity with the poor and the oppressed while maintaining critical distance from partisan engagement in politics.

The sin of apartheid led to such immoral exclusion and bloodshed encompassing innocent South Africans that the yearning for freedom and liberation from the yoke of oppression could be realized only by the acts of solidarity between the global moral community and the local ecumenical movement. Hence, as in the case of South Africa, global and local ecumenical initiatives become the nexus between sacred and secular advancements in the search for solutions to the dilemmas facing Africa.

3. MEMORY AND SOCIAL RESPONSIBILITY

Another example of ecumenical social responsibility in which the churches and civil society have come together is the historic Ufungamano initiative in Kenya. The building was a shelter for forces of change under the auspices of the ecumenical movement in Kenya. It is a place of social memory for the role that the churches have played together with other faith-based and civil society groups including political parties in Kenya. The churches have to accompany one another in the journey to find solutions to the problems facing our people. New theological insights and methods of understanding the complexities of global and local political arrangements are becoming increasingly essential.

The churches in Africa must continue to provide the moral space for the growth of the ecumenical movement through such initiatives that bring together Christians, Muslims and people of other faiths. There are three critical areas that summarize the active life of the ecumenical movement in social and political transition in Africa. The areas may be categorized as discernment, moral formation, and peace-building. Most of the countries in which the ecumenical social responsibility became the guiding paradigm were either going through democratic transition or were on the verge of political and social upheaval.

The institutional claims of unity or the search for unity are constantly called into question by our lack of immediate and adequate preventive responses to the unceasing conflicts on the continent. Indigenous modes of consensus-building and the institutions of moral authority are often left out in the search for lasting solutions to the problems facing Africa. The configuration of nation-state boundaries and attempts to create regional frontiers of co-operation in trade and industry still do not facilitate adequate free movement and cultural exchange between peoples of the same heritage in the continent. Unfortunately the endeavours for secular unity are largely hindered by the legacy of foreign languages and bureaucratic structures. Ecumenical unity is not possible without the language of diversity genuinely being grounded in the desire for unity. Therefore the various languages and cultures of the African people must be in dialogue beyond the colonial identity motifs that they tend to represent. Why should Africans quarrel in meetings over the superiority of European languages when it is possible to develop the use of Kiswahili, for example?

Participants in the Thanksgiving service at St Andrews Church.

Today our common challenge in the ecumenical movement is to develop alternative measures and methodologies for comprehensive understanding of the prevailing conditions that lead to conflicts in the continent. While poverty and disease are on the increase in most parts of the continent, struggles for the well-being of the poor and the weak must remain at the top of our agenda together. But above all we need the capacity for truth-telling as part and parcel of the process of the healing of memories. The culture of truth-telling is the only way that we shall facilitate an honest and confident process of healing of memories. Healing is an essential part of the life and work of the church. Healing and forgiveness are interconnected, and they are an integral part of our Christian vocation.

4. HEALING OF MEMORIES

We cannot neglect our past; the memory will always remain with us, but we can heal and reconcile our memory. Reconciliation is based on forgiveness, and forgiveness must be based on confession. Therefore, it is confession that generates healing and forgiveness. We at the WCC do not believe in a cheap forgiveness and reconciliation. The truth must be told and accepted and then, and only then, memory shall be respected. The classical image of the church is that of a healing community. Jesus Christ's main ministry apart from preaching and teaching about the kingdom of God was healing. He was compassionate towards the sick and suffering of this world. Since most churches have the invaluable social network and moral capital to intervene in any human crisis, they must begin to set an example in the case of Rwanda. Time is of the essence for the churches to strengthen their place as a healing community.

Again, it is the heads of churches together with civil society institutions that can pre-empt the re-emergence of genocide in Africa. The church has a very unique role in creating space for restorative justice where the oppressors and the oppressed come together in a dialogue of inter-action. The ultimate aim of restorative justice is healing and reconciliation. The churches should promote the kind of juridical–legal system where preventive, punitive and restorative justice are combined for the transformation of the whole society.

The ancestors teach us that we must listen to this earth and feel the pulse of life. But we cannot do that if we are estranged from each other and therefore cannot recognize our connection to the sacred nature of life. In Africa we believe that the world is a living shrine because human life directly depends upon it and its vital forces. The earth is our home, and the prolongation of the life of human beings is ultimately bound to the earth's fecundity. The sky, the earth and all the living and breathing things that give life and balance to the cosmos are essential to our being in the world. Therefore the ushering in of a New World is organically related with the struggles to change the very world in which we live (see *The Courage to Hope* by the Rev. Dr Samuel Kobia, Risk Books – WCC Publications, 2003).

The truth is that human beings cannot create, or even imagine, anything that is entirely new in history. Everything we do is predicated by something else in history. But in Christ, behold, everything has been renewed and, as we often say theologically, our encounter with him is the encounter with truth. But it is not an abstract truth. It is the social and spiritual truth that we experience in the work we do to build the kingdom of God, and in sharing the eucharistic meal something new always happens

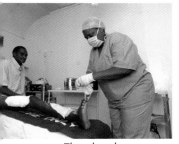

The churches support ministries of healthcare and healing.

in the community of believers. Christ, in whose suffering our suffering as a community of faith is embodied, becomes for us both the object and the promise of the new moral eschatological community.

As the apostle Paul instructs in his pastoral letters, once incorporated into the body one is expected to live according to the mind of Christ. Thus we support a truth-telling culture in order to bring health to the life of the body. Activities within the body of Christ produce a new group identity and a Christ-filled worldview. Paul skilfully appropriated the prevailing social vision of his time to name a new ecumenical reality of faith that included both the Gentiles and the "believers" into one new "body" without undermining but re-negotiating the essential foundations of faith.

5. THE BODY OF CHRIST AND THE COSMOS

At the same time we must remember that the body of Christ extends to the body of the cosmos. For example, the outcome of the rage of genocide may even affect life in the natural world, as in the case of Rwanda. When poverty and apathy become the defining mode of relations in a community, then a trigger of hatred could easily lead to an endless chain of violence with impunity. "When I came out, there were no birds," said one survivor who had hidden throughout the genocide in Rwanda. "There was sunshine and the stench of death." The dread of genocidal death by any other name is not just death, if even the birds in the air can escape from the rooftops and watch helplessly at a distance as human beings slaughter each other with machetes. Not only the birds, but the rest of creation was stunned by the genocide in Rwanda. It is said that the sun was shy to shine on that day, and the twilight was transformed by an aurora coloured with blood! In order to restore harmony in the community we must begin with a process of facing the truth of the events as they took place. And there is no place other than the church where this process can begin and come to fruition.

6. CONCLUSION

The World Council of Churches is committed to accompanying the churches and the ecumenical movement in Africa through a process in which conscientization becomes part of collective reflection that will strengthen the church as the effective instrument of radical social transformation. The rights of the victims of genocide must be affirmed as those owed to a special people and members of the moral community. The church should be made to understand itself as a compassionate, loving, just and caring community. The ethical and moral imperatives of justice towards displaced persons and victims of genocide must be made a priority in the healing process. The best models, practices and responses to conflicts in Africa ought to be tested and shared ecumenically.

The church as the body of Christ must acknowledge through her leadership that when the members are afflicted by genocide, the church too is afflicted and wounded. Hence the need to transform the church into a living community of hope for both the victims and victimizers, a moral space in which confession and forgiveness becomes possible. The commitment of the church in alleviating suffering and the space it provides for moral formation must be affirmed by the ecumenical movement. The people of Africa have come a long way seeking to live with dignity, and therefore this pastoral visit by the most senior officers of the World Council of Churches is an affirmation that the whole ecumenical family not only walks with Africa but also learns how God continues to do wonderful things among her people.

Increasingly women provide leadership in the African churches.

7

BEHOLD I CREATE A NEW AFRICA

1. INTRODUCTION

Several years ago, as a young man seeking to fathom what the future might hold for me, and which path I might want to pursue in life, I was awakened by the Socratic dictum that "the unexamined life is not worth living". And my choice of re-examination of life led me to the values and truths embedded in theological inquiry. The place where my formation as an aspiring theologian and ecumenist began was at St Paul's Theological College in Limuru. Hence, the legacy of this great college has remained part of my own professional and pastoral journey at the World Council of Churches.

In this lecture I shall endeavour to re-examine the place of Africa in the world and her destiny beyond colonial memory. I will begin with a brief critique of Paul's theology as it relates to State Authority and then proceed to provide several affirmations based on a deeper theological and philosophical critique of African Identity. My approach is both analytic and hermeneutic, but at the same time allows room for a more spontaneous outpouring of new and old ideas as they unfold. However, at the heart of this inquiry, which I share with a number of scholars, is the critical question of authenticity of theology both as a system of knowledge and as a vision for humanity in the context of the African experience.

The people of the churches labour together with dedication.

2. NO CONCESSION TO ANY FORM OF TYRANNY

BY THE REV. DR SAMUEL KOBIA

We must embrace the great responsibility bequeathed us by the societies and people of Africa. Interpretations of the biblical texts by theologians have always been the occasion for political and social discourses that either affirm or undermine the prophetic vocation and relationship between the Church and the State. We should never give leaders in Africa the opportunity to play politics with the lives of people. Let me begin for example with a very brief critique of a controversial hermeneutic of Paul's theology based on the famous passage of Romans 13:1-7, which suggests that all authority comes from God! Every theological position defines a political and social location of the church. The theology of apartheid for example was based not only on a false anthropology but also on very controversial biblical hermeneutics. Reading into scripture, power without the authority of the people may be legitimated (Rom. 13:1-7), as may the enforcement of an unethical regime in the name of "Law and Order". Blind obedience and absolute loyalty to tyranny come to be equated with civic and theological virtues of the state. The text of Paul is then the definitive doctrine that bequeaths state authority through theological instruments of unlimited power. The text is often interpreted out of context, and a new meaning is derived that distorts its social location.

Formation within the churches helps to shape the future.

Paul was obviously writing to a particular Christian community in Rome, which was faced with peculiar problems in relation to state authority. What may appear to be an appeal for absolute obedience to state authority and a claim that all authority is derived from God is not an ontological justification for oppression; neither is it a moral concession for tyranny. Then what is it? The community to which the text of Paul refers was that of enthusiasts who believed that only Christians were exonerated from obeying any State and that somehow they were above the law because Jesus alone was their Lord and King.

This heretical position obviously had major political consequences, which would compel Paul to proclaim that before the second coming, Christians are part of the world and under the same rules of governance that regulate secular life. Paul is here not concerned about the power of the state or the epistemology of authority as such; rather, given the level of enthusiasm with the authority of Jesus over "divine and secular matters", it was necessary for Paul to give a balancing perspective on the relationship between civic public life and Christian identity.

Furthermore, in late antiquity and Hellenistic times, both Jews and Christians had rejected the notion that imperial authority of the Romans,

Egyptians, Babylonians or Greeks was absolute and of divine origin. The apocalyptic description of these empires in the biblical texts, e.g. the books of Daniel and Revelation contradict the hermeneutics of state authority derived from Romans 13:1-7. To use this text outside its context in order to authenticate the reign of tyrants and despots is to commit both theological and political heresy.

The question of spiritual authority versus the use of other forms of power which are unethical must continue to be made subject to theological reflection, and this merits the attention of the church. African theology must focus not only on the nature of being but must also become practical and incarnational at the heart of Christian identity. In Luke 4:18–19 and John 10:10, Jesus describes and defines his humanity in terms of bringing happiness and fulfilment to human life. He came that we might have life, and have it abundantly. In these struggles the mission and calling of the churches together is to usher in a bountiful new dispensation of abundant life. To restore the fragmented humanity of the African people will not only take alternative political institutions to the normative discourse of the market but also a new revolution of the heart. As we experience healing from within even the institutions to which we belong, we realize in the process that the ultimate goal of healing is to restore the distinctive identity and dignity of the African people. Our theological endeavours must express the depth of the quest for healing and restoration and inspire the emergence of new organic moral communities in Africa.

The method of doing theology must therefore be sensitive to the migration of ideas and biases that do not constitute the life and experience of the communities in which the text was produced. If the hermeneutic is flawed then theological claims will often misinterpret the message of the text. I would therefore want to make a shift to an area of inquiry where not much reflection has been made, yet it is the realm where African theologians can play a leading role.

In this struggle for authenticity to seek the face of God in the midst of the contradictions that we encounter in our history as Africans, we must brace not just for the obvious but for the extraordinary. The suffering and struggles born out of negative history do not make us entirely hostage to the logic of anguish; neither should we surrender to the global and local forces of tyranny if we are to be faithful to the claim that our God is the Lord of history.

As the continent and her peoples are constantly under cultural siege and perpetually being mutilated by predatory forces of conquest, we must remember that our hope is embedded in vigilance with the Word of God which speaks to us in the spirits of our ancestors, and ultimately is revealed in the exemplary life and value of the Jesus narrative. It is in solidarity with the suffering, determination to live with the dying and celebration of the resurrection to new life, that Jesus becomes for us the living motif of hope in Africa.

Those of us who have succumbed to the vestiges of social, political and spiritual re-assignment must know that the world cannot be at peace with itself without Africa. The hope for the liberation of this world is not possible if Africa is engulfed in anguish. This is so simply because the soul of Africa is endowed not only with the vortex of the human spirit but also the vital force of life in the universe.

The soul of Africa is the soul of the world. The life-giving spirit of God which visits us in healing moments and consoles us in times of great tribulation nourishes the soul of Africa by making her sons and daughters become the beacon of a new dream for an ever-emerging renewal in Africa. The classical image of the church is that of a healing community. Jesus Christ's main ministry apart from preaching and teaching about the kingdom of God was healing. He was compassionate towards the sick and suffering of this world. Since most churches have a long history in dealing with health issues in the continent, a coordinated outreach effort by the churches together is eagerly awaited. Time is of extreme essence for the churches to reclaim their place as a healing community. Pastoral care, emo-

3. QUEST FOR AUTHENTICITY

tional support and living with God spiritually and with human beings socially is so important in dealing with the spread of HIV/AIDS among the youth.

A new generation of children born today under the yoke of the HIV/AIDS pandemic will give Africa new insights into the journey of the cross and the momentous awakening of the human spirit that transcends the confusions of finitude which even the western world is ill-equipped to deal with.

When science informs our understanding of the visible world, and philosophy bequeaths us the capacity to comprehend the structure of reality, theology has become for us the handmaid of all inquiries because in theology we are engaged in thinking about everything at all times! In theology we are engaged in thinking about thinking! To think of everything is only possible because God envelopes our thoughts with contemplative compassion and insight into the true meaning of our existence in this world. Therefore, in order to make any meaningful breakthrough in the theological reflections of whichever kind we must engage, every field of inquiry and every claim of normative discourse must be subjected to the reality of God's intervening historical presence and how that presence reforms and reclaims human destiny.

The Orthodox Church is growing throughout Africa.

The colonial memory has remained our mode of engaging the primordial self, yet the reality that informs who we really are, even unconsciously, has nothing to do with our preoccupation with colonial memory. Africa is the protagonist of human origins inherited from the primordial legacy of humankind. African history is larger than antiquity because she produced the Greek and the Mediterranean world that created Europe, even as she has embraced modernity complete with its vicissitudes. Africa is a continent of historical contradictions because she produces a world that is estranged from her own soul. The search for an authentic vision of African Christianity must therefore take into account the ambiguities of these burdens of history that spill over into Africa through colonial memory.

This vision explains our critical endeavour to create ecumenical space in which churches in Africa may begin to reflect and respond in solidarity with one another beyond the colonial moments that produced them, so that the people of Africa begin not to be preoccupied with the attempt to repair those historical moments, but rather to live beyond them with this new rekindling vision of life. How do we invoke the hidden memories of survival in stories and songs that will continue to nurture the spirit of the African people? Where is the dignifying value of African humanity to be found and how subtle is the expression of it even in the midst of great suffering and confusion? Such questions should guide our renewed desire to awaken not just what has been lost but rather what can be found in the encounter and struggles of the ordinary people in the continent.

A degree of optimism in this regard arises from the sociability in characterizing the African value system, and a capacity for joy that defies empirical statistics on poverty, suffering, apathy and death. The capacity to face without denial the mutilation of identity in colonial history must be admitted if we are to unlock the energies hidden by oppression. The wounding of the continent through the ugly history of long suffering and fragmentation of her humanity cannot be set right simply by a fresh start through a resurgence of superficial political projects. This wounding of the continent must lead us to ask, what are the values of African culture and the depth of humanity that permitted Africans to survive?

As part of her mission and calling the church is called not only to prepare citizens to participate in national elections but also to equip them with instruments of discernment and foresight on not only how to elect but also to reject the kind of leadership that is oppressive. It is her mandate to ensure that people inform their collective behaviour and action, in the same way as they inform their individual actions and behaviour. Otherwise, the church can no longer be the salt nor the guiding light on the hill. Ethical discernment with a clear coherent understanding of the contemporary trends in the continent

4. THE DEPTH OF OUR HUMANITY

5. ETHICAL DISCERNMENT AND SOCIAL RESPONSIBILITY

"Work and prayer" in the rebuilding of Africa.

will provide the framework of engagement in all spheres of public life for and on behalf of the churches and peoples of Africa. The prophetic vision of the church as the conscience of society must inform her of every action on behalf of the working poor. Critical solidarity with the victims of violence and advocacy against all the oppressive forces operating in the continent must inform our theological endeavours towards a new ecclesiology. The visibility of the continental ecumenical movement mirrored and articulated though the programmatic vision of the All Africa Conference of Churches, for example, must therefore reflect the intrinsic value of African theologies of advocacy.

At the World Council of Churches we realize that Africa is on the threshold of new boundaries of global and local realities, and you have the means to redefine who you are and even reclaim your place as Africans beyond that which has been lost by history. Our hope is anchored in the fact that you and we at the WCC are not alone. So long as our commitment is connected to the transforming power of the grandeur of God in all creation, we shall be empowered to change the conditions of depravity and alienation that produce anguish and misery among our people. Africa must arise now and with renewed vigour reclaim her new place in the world.

6. AFRICAN DESTINY AND CHRISTIAN IDENTITY

Unlike the 20th century which was dominated by the politics of ideology, the 21st century will be dominated by the politics of identity. Given the fact that religion is a powerful source of identity, human conflicts and projects of conquest are likely to gain ontological justification. The invention of ideological boundaries and the reinvention of new motifs of the self may create more complexities that, if we are not careful, may lead to further mutilation of vulnerable communities.

The question of identity as a social construction in naming the other is often based on power relations in the western sense. The matrix of identity is politically designed and hidden by the power of naming. The subject is often objectified as exclusively distinct with claims of privileged identity on the part of the naming agency. The rhetoric of civilizing results ultimately in the naming of otherness. I have longed to understand why a people would indulge so much in a project of unleashing violence while remaining unconscious of their wrong-doing, so that violence becomes for them the instrument by which they zealously engage in a mission to civilize and convert "others" to their values and way of life. This is what makes race and the ideology of racism a foundational construction of identity even though in ethical terms it is the most illegitimate, illusive and inhuman way of naming otherness.

Education is taken seriously by the churches.

After the protracted struggles during the civil rights movement, even in America we are not anywhere near resolving the racial problem. The international question of equity and historical justice for Africans in the diaspora with respect to racism is no longer a question that can be faced with legal nomenclature. However, how can we address the power of naming without the language to name who we are? If we name each other in languages that do not belong to us, then how authentic is our vision of life? These are very deep moral questions that go to the very essence of what it really means to be human. We must also ask the question, by whose memory do we understand who we really are as Africans? The way in which we name our world has a lot to do with systems and structures of rekindling memory. Hence the colonial enterprise was largely a project of erasing memory.

In racism, the naming of identity takes place as an act that is both anti-human and by necessity anti-God. Yet the violence of words camouflaged in the triumph of a world that belongs to the other, a world whose meaning has been superimposed onto other worlds as if there were no other worlds before it – is the essential violence that still looms among us today. I am more profoundly aware than at any other time of the need to be equipped with more subtle analytical instruments to decipher and discern the complexities of the global enterprise of naming and being named by virtue of how much you own or are owned by the other. In the global process of economic naming the poor are continually being punished with impunity and the rich are rewarded with liquidity. The fate of groups within western culture and civilization in late modernity is bound by the naming of otherness.

The dilemma we face in Africa today is what to do with the tools of analysis acquired through the conquest narrative (formal education) without turning our backs on education. It is like asking the question, if someone who is oppressive tells you the Bible teaches that you should love your neighbour, how should you respond? Obviously not with a kind of "love" that allows oppression to flourish or that which sanctions powerlessness. The world is yearning for a new revolution of consciousness that transcends the naming systems. The stones and walls that came down with the end of colonialism did not signify the end of a season of confusion, nor did the new colours hide the memories of a crime. Truth is revealed in segments of time until the new day of fuller emancipation is announced. Oftentimes we have to wait a long time for healing to come because memories replay with new images distorting actual events in the past.

7. WHENCE SHALL JUSTICE FLOW WITH PEACE?

The proponents of the theology of reconstruction rightly argue that historically the motif of liberation bears the historical burden of struggle out of confinement. Yet at the heart of the liberation struggle is not just a preoccupation with territoriality and reclaiming of spaces that we once occupied! Liberation is essentially a process of reclaiming the authentic self and becoming free from the naming chains of this world. That there has been in Africa a movement away from the land of oppression, and constant engagement out of the crisis of victimhood, is only a half truth. The historical juxtaposition of the biblical narrative of liberation with colonial and post-colonial histories of struggle in Africa, as if providing a clear and neat paradigm, seems to me a little too simplistic. Our understanding of the events in recent African history as representing obvious parallels to biblical hermeneutics must be questioned. We must defy every attempt to simplify the complexities in our journey towards a new Africa where justice and peace flow like a river and abundant life is a reality for all people.

The transition from colonial rule to the crafting of the modern bifurcated nation–state in Africa does not represent a neat historical progression from liberation to a biblical pattern of reconstruction. In this regard there is constant interplay between liberation and reconstruction, but with a thrust of optimism concerning the reinvention of a New Africa! Debate on the need for paradigm shifts away from normative understandings of "official" theological discourse, and global mapping of Africa, must continue. Only a comprehensive theological vision that incorporates the memories of the ordinary experiences and struggles of the African people will succeed in this project of reinventing a New Africa.

The question of identity has always been central to both African philosophy and theology. From the works of John S. Mbiti to Kwame Bediako, Kä Mana Kangudie and Musa W. Dube, just to name a few, there is real intellectual zeal and capacity for imagination which transcend philological categories and analytical systems based on western jurisprudence. The intellectual industry of some African scholars is superior and invites serious consideration of alternative epistemological categories in doing theology. Obviously there are problems with certain aspects of Mbiti's work, especially when it comes to the question of the African concept of time. However, this does not in any way minimize his pioneering work in African theological scholarship. Rather, we now have an appreciation of the complexities of myriad African cosmologies, even as we seek one holistic view combining the existential with the metaphysical.

Dance expresses the spirit of celebration in worship.

Kwame Bediako's work affirms the vision of authenticity especially as it relates to the need for enculturation and re-articulation of alternative images and motifs of Jesus that are relevant to Africa today. Such motifs must relate to the structure of ordinary experience and the spirituality of ordinary people in Africa. Indeed Prof. Kwesi Dickson of Ghana described the phenomenon of ordinary spirituality as "fellow-feeling with nature". The mysterious powers of faith are at work in the ordinary narratives and struggles of daily living among the poor and the silenced majority in Africa. Ka Mana's depth theology, if I may call it that, seeks to excavate the depth of African creativity with a poetic imagination that endeavours to recover our lost historical self from the dungeons of post-colonial modernism.

His work, though sometimes criticized as nostalgic, represents to theology what the negritude movement represents to African philosophy. The histories of African encounter with the Middle Eastern and Mediterranean worlds which informed earlier thinking in the continent are largely ignored by the intellectual mapping of the continent informed only by the most recent post-colonial encounters. The latter produced the kind of living jurisprudence that in many ways is still hostile to the original structures of thought and engagement defined by African scholars. The soul of Africa has been engulfed but not destroyed by these hegemonic forces. This is because Africa retains not only by virtue of her primordial origins but also in her designs for the future the more complex existential phenomenon which I named earlier as "the vortex of the human spirit". The inner life of suffering people that preserves their dignity in the face of suffering reveals something that cannot be put into words but which is connected to the heart of being.

8. THE SPIRITUAL HOME OF CHRISTIANITY

The historical burden is upon us as scholars and theologians not just to prove the obvious but to re-affirm the inevitable; our responsibility is to the whole human race, because we have been touched by God on behalf of humanity. The question of dignity of the human person before God and the reality of alienation from the goodness of creation are critical for African theology. We must explain these contradictions because they bear the existential burden that calls into question the very essence of theology. The epistemological framework within which we do theology must be informed and re-inform the social, political and scientific cultures that prevail in our world.

A famous Jesuit mystic and paleontologist, Teilhard de Chardin, on the eve of the Second World War wrote a memorable passage about how silently man had made his entry upon the scene of global history.

"He trod so softly that when his presence was at last betrayed by the indestructible evidence of his stone tool, he was already spread across the Ancient World from the Cape of Good Hope to Peking".

But that was before the excavations around Lake Turkana, the unearthing of Lucy. The primordial beginnings of life in Africa as revealed by contemporary empirical evidence based largely on recent scientific findings invite us to re-think the western biblical models of creation and begin a new intellectual path suggesting an alternative theological hermeneutics of human origins. While so much work based on the nostalgic philosophy of the negritude movement has already been accomplished, linking Africa to an alternative thought system, the making of historical claims for Egyptian civilization as the source of African currents in the flow of global history has only just begun.

There is so much yet to be done in reclaiming the specificity of Africa's place in the context of contemporary events and scientific findings. As the birthplace of the human race, the ultimate destiny of Africa ought to be reconfigured around engagement with contemporary global realities. By about 20,000 years ago the transition to Late Stone Age industries was virtually complete all over Africa. And then there was the Ethiopian kingdom of Aksum, which had become a city-state by the first century AD, and had its first encounter with Christianity in the fourth century. I conclude that Africa is not only our primordial home but essentially the spiritual home of Christianity. It is now generally accepted that by 2040 the centre of Christianity will have shifted to Africa. The question we must ask is what kind of Christianity it is going to be. And what kind of moral responsibility will Africa bear towards the rest of the Christendom and the world, by virtue of being the centre of Christianity?

Samuel Kobia with Bishop Paul of the Coptic Church.

9. CONCLUSION

My dear Africa, your time has come. Henceforth, stop agonizing and apologizing to the world about who you are, or even reminding the world about your need to be affirmed through the history of those who enslaved you and oppressed you by the very cruelty of their own ideology and institutions! It is time for you to be awakened by the resources of your own soul and yield to the invisible hand of God who has walked with you during your moments of great affliction.

The magnificent one, the Creator of the heavens and the earth, to whom everything submits with gratitude, says to you today, from the ashes of your harsh history and the wealth of innocence bestowed upon your Children, Behold I create a new Africa even with the invisible hand unseen amid the structures of evidence known to human sight! I create a new moment in which your responsibility is far greater than the despondency of your affliction.

Furthermore I hear God saying that "I bring upon Africa a new rebirth of the Spirit, full of equanimity which overflows with new joy that derides every anguish of the children of Africa and brings them to the brink of a new wakeful moment of courage and hope." Then I see the future when Africans in the diaspora will accompany us. And together we will affirm that Africa, as the primordial home of humanity, will rise to the occasion and take leadership in the struggle to create a new world in which all will live as good neighbours to each other. With confidence, with intellectual and theological competence, we shall work hand in hand with one another to prepare for the new dawn of the kingdom of God upon the people of Africa.

8 DO NOT BE AFRAID, PEOPLE OF RWANDA

1. INTRODUCTION

Rwanda has been wounded. She lives with the memories that silence our desire for hope. And just as the disciples had grown weary because of the sad events of their time, we too can become captive to the events that reflect the emptiness of the tomb. We saw for ourselves the tomb of Rwanda. Where the innocent citizens, including children, lay in utter silence. Weary, wretched by the weight of our sins, Jesus had been hung on the cross as the climax of a journey of pain and humiliation. He was abandoned to die alone while his disciples had grown weary and been overcome with fear. They even considered abandoning the mission and values for which Jesus lived and gave up his life. He was wounded for no fault of his own yet stricken in his own heart for the sake of the dignity of every human being. In critical years of his young life Jesus found a home in Africa where he came as a refugee. And in his journey towards the cross, it was an African, Simon of Cyrene, who helped Jesus bear the weight of the burden of humanity. Africans helped carry the cross of Jesus to Calvary. Jesus has a special place for Africa in his heart, and that is why he still comes to us and chooses to reveal himself to ordinary people and especially to those excluded in our society.

Silent prayer and meditation at the Kigali genocide memorial.

2. THE TRUTH OF JESUS WILL HEAL YOU

Like the disciples of Jesus we have experienced the fear of the unknown. But the women, who on the first day of the week longed to see Jesus, left their homes and outran each other with eagerness to have a glimpse of the tomb. They too were in haste, not knowing what was awaiting them. First the angel of God breaks the news to Mary Magdalene and the other Mary, who couldn't have slept well enough because they knew they had a duty to their Lord who lay in the tomb for a third day. Then, within moments of their encounter with the angel, Jesus himself – now resurrected from the dead – goes on

BY THE REV. DR SAMUEL KOBIA

to say, "Do not be afraid". Even death was silenced at the cross and Jesus lives today among us; therefore, we need not live in fear. Now let us look at the behaviour of the women after they heard those words of accompaniment.

They left the tomb not with fear but with joy to go and tell the good news to the disciples. Nobody could stop them anymore. And this may have been the greatest moment of all times, the birth of the Christian faith and Christianity. The women of the resurrection were the first to be called witnesses of our faith.

Consider for a moment the role of witnesses. Witnesses have seen it, and can tell it as it was, for they are the custodians of authentic memory and have the authority to relive what happened. They live to tell the story so that the truth may live on. They have this noble responsibility of being custodians of the truth. And it is to them that the angel of God and Jesus had this to say: Do not be afraid. Do not be afraid even when the past is coloured with gloom because you no longer live in the past. Do not be afraid of the unforeseen because even the future belongs to God. Today Jesus says to the people of Rwanda, "Do not fret, neither be weighed down by the burden of your history. Cast all your fears away, for I am with you; do not be afraid. Be a witness to courage, faith and the embrace of the truth of the resurrection".

3. PEACE BE WITH YOU (JOHN 20:19)

After the suffering and the death of Jesus the disciples locked themselves in a room out of fear, not knowing what to do or how to relate to the world. They were faced with the very dilemma of continuity in the aftermath of the untold suffering and death of Jesus.

They were tiptoeing at the brink of despair with many questions whose answers the world could not give. In much the same state the people of Rwanda find themselves, even ten years later after the genocide. The nation has been engulfed with memories of anguish and pain. However, just as the sudden appearance of Jesus with the message of peace surprised the disciples into joy, so it is that the history which has been locked up with memories of genocide will break free into a new future of prosperity

God's gift of children affirms life.

for the people of Rwanda. And with the confidence of faith we have embarked on a journey together with you, hand in hand, to embrace the authentic peace which this world cannot give. This is the kind of peace that endures through all times and awakens in us the confidence that no matter what happens and in whichever condition we find ourselves, the hand of God will never let go of us. Peace is therefore the holistic fulfilment of all endeavours that are in harmony with God's intention for the world. Peace is also the experience of inner calm and contentment of being which flourishes in our encounter with life.

The contemplative joy that comes out of our encounter with Jesus awakens in us the enthusiasm to transform the world and the way we relate to each other. When Jesus came into this world, he came in the name of peace. The angelic greetings to the peasants and shepherds of Palestine contained a wish for peace to all men and women of goodwill. In his final greeting to the disciples Jesus offered them peace as a gift of the resurrection. From the suffering and death of Jesus we are awakened to the kind of peace which this world cannot give.

Again I say to you that the people of Rwanda who died violently followed in the innocent footsteps of Jesus. Today we see the consequences of pain and suffering among those who survived the genocide; they too walked with Jesus to the cross. Their anguish, like the anguish of Job, is a yearning to find answers to the meaning of life in the midst of unfathomable contradictions. Yet in this life as in death, Jesus himself comes to fill our anguish with his presence, and he responds to our silent cry with the profound gift of his risen presence. Jesus waits at the door of every home, every government corridor and every street in Rwanda with the gift of peace.

There are among us many young people in Rwanda today who live with the desire to be safe and who seek an assurance of a new future worth our endurance. They seek to belong again to a peaceable community founded on justice.

May this be the occasion when all the children of Rwanda find solace in our confidence in the possibility of re-building this great nation! Let us look beyond the memories of unthinkable violence in which all were scattered by the sword of death and immersed in the conditions of darkness, as if our lives were meant to be measured by endless toil. Bidden or not bidden, Jesus is present and our consolation is that we are not and will never be alone even when we are engulfed in what seems to be total abandonment. Let us arise, wounded people of Rwanda, and be overjoyed just like the disciples of Jesus, and once again let us pave the way for the new dawn of the kingdom of God upon future generations in Africa.

4. CONCLUSION

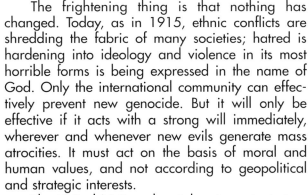

GENOCIDES IN THE 20TH CENTURY

1. INTRODUCTION

The 20th century was an age of genocide, and the list is depressingly long: Armenians, Jews, Cambodians, Kurds, Tutsi, Croats, Muslims and Albanians. The international community was always slow to respond to these mass killings, and in some cases it simply ignored them. My people were victims of the first genocide of the 20th century. One-and-a-half million Armenians were massacred in a well-planned and systematic programme of killing by the Turkish government during the First World War. We Armenians know, out of our existential and painful experience, all about the far-reaching consequences of genocide.

2. TOWARDS THE PREVENTION OF GENOCIDE

The frightening thing is that nothing has changed. Today, as in 1915, ethnic conflicts are shredding the fabric of many societies; hatred is hardening into ideology and violence in its most horrible forms is being expressed in the name of God. Only the international community can effectively prevent new genocide. But it will only be effective if it acts with a strong will immediately, wherever and whenever new evils generate mass atrocities. It must act on the basis of moral and human values, and not according to geopolitical and strategic interests.

The United Nations has taken important steps in its attempt to prevent genocide. It ratified the Genocide Convention in 1948 and followed that immediately with the Declaration of Human Rights. In 1998, 120 states established the International Criminal Court (ICC) in The Hague, The Netherlands, which has jurisdiction over genocide, crimes against humanity and war crimes. These are good steps. But they have not accomplished their main aim; they have not prevented genocide. The ICC's attention is on the crime that has been committed and not on the crime that must be prevented, and the international community must go beyond these juridical commitments and processes.

One of many Rwandan cemeteries where approximately one million victims of the genocide lie buried.

BY HIS HOLINESS ARAM I

It must impose its political will in positive ways; it must create early warning systems, and build public awareness, education and dialogue. Wherever applicable, it should impose diplomatic and economic sanctions and in extreme situations, when all else has failed, engage in humanitarian intervention.

Individually and collectively, people live with memory, and memory lives through them. Memory links the present to the past and conditions the future, thereby ensuring continuity and affirming identity. Collective memory is history. Nations are formed around their common memory. It sustains their existence, maintains their unity and gives them a sense of belonging. Collective memory tells the untold history of a people; it is a living source of truth. It challenges bias and partial information and builds awareness. With this awareness comes the possibility of accepting or calling for responsibility.

Only when we become aware and accept responsibility can we move to repentance, forgiveness and reconciliation. With genocide this process is crucial. Wipe out the memory and you wipe out the possibility of justice. Leave the untold story untold and you will never stop the cycle of violence. Leave people unaware and they will be that much more easily victimized. Hitler understood this well. He used the fate of the Armenians at the hands of the Turks in 1915 to justify his plans for extermination. He knew that memories were short. "Who today," he asked, "remembers the genocide of the Armenians." Well, today, some people, for political motives, do not "remember the genocide of the Armenians"; others refer to it as an "alleged" genocide. The Armenian people, however, live the memory of genocide vividly in their daily life. That memory is deeply rooted in their collective consciousness. Is this not true also of the Rwandan people? You have so many painful experiences, so many stories of violence and images of suffering that must be shared with others, not as an expression of hate and intolerance, but as a challenge to move to repentance, forgiveness and reconciliation.

3. MEMORY AS A SOURCE OF TRUTH

Coptic sisters organize social ministries in the community.

4. RECOGNITION AS THE WAY TOWARDS JUSTICE

The truth that is preserved by memory must also be told: "No one after lighting a lamp puts it under the bushel basket, but on the lamp stand, and it gives light to all in the house" (Matthew 5: 15). Only then will that truth be recognized. If it is not recognized, there will be denial, because without recognition there can be no awareness and without awareness there can be no responsibility and accountability. Any individual, community or government that does not recognize and then accept responsibility for genocide commits a crime against humanity. To accept the truth of genocide and the responsibility for it takes great courage and does not come easily. It can only result from a process of self-critical reflection, a search for self-understanding.

The individual, community or government must reread their history in an inter-relational context. Only through such a self-assessing, self-critical and self-purifying process will the truth become clear. Different truth and reconciliation committees that have been established provide the space in which the difficult experience of self-criticism and the understanding of truth are being discussed by victim and offender together. These new models, which have embodied the Christian imperative that confession is a pre-condition for justice and reconciliation, have been partially successful, and we must build on them. We must avoid models that are guided by political agendas; often, governments will refuse to acknowledge that crimes have been committed and will, therefore, not accept responsibility for them. In the 20th century some cases of genocide have been acknowledged and others have been denied. Where they have been acknowledged, communities and nations are moving towards justice and reconciliation. Where they have been denied, the wound of injustice is still festering.

5. IMPUNITY: CONTINUOUS GENOCIDE

In situations where communities or governments will not acknowledge and take responsibility for genocide, justice may only be achieved through a punitive approach. However, according to many jurists, existing criminal systems and juridical procedures emphasize the criminal and not the victim;

in this way, the courts attempt to affirm human rights and promote justice by punishing the criminal. However, real justice can happen only when the rights of the victim are strongly recognized and addressed as well.

Restorative justice is a new development in the criminal system. It opens new dimensions in both the preventive and punitive approaches. It is a victim-centred system. Restorative justice aims to restore dialogue by bringing together the offender and the victim for reconciliation. The Truth and Reconciliation Commission of South Africa is a concrete example of this process. Restorative justice must also include retributive justice. The first generates healing by creating space for dialogue, and the second leads to community building and reconciliation. For there to be true justice and accountability, there must be reparation, restitution and compensation for the victims.

Punitive measures through the ICC and the new paradigms arising from the truth and reconciliation committees are essential to avoid continuous genocide, because impunity perpetuates injustice, which, in turn, generates acts of revenge in an endless cycle of violence. It also generates new forms of injustice and violations of human rights. Offenders should be held accountable to humanity. Many offenders have not yet been brought to justice and held accountable for their acts. Impunity means granting de facto amnesty. If we can bring single criminals routinely to justice, why can't we bring governments or nations to justice as well?

Life and joy radiate from the smiling faces of the young.

Some of the genocides of the 20th century have been recognized and retribution has been made. For example, in Rwanda retributive justice is being established both through the United Nations and through the government and people of Rwanda. However, the Armenian genocide remains unpunished. Restorative justice could be the model both for the Armenian genocide and for other crimes against humanity still awaiting justice.

6. CONCLUSION

Respect for human rights is crucial to any process aimed at the restoration of justice, permanent peace and reconciliation. Over the past 56 years, the United Nations has sought to implement the Universal Declaration on Human Rights by adopting international covenants related to specific areas of human rights, including genocide. However, these attempts have not prevented millions of people from falling victim to atrocity, repression and genocide. Again and again, governments have ignored their commitments to these covenants, bypassed them and acted unilaterally. The cries of the victims of human rights violations still are heard all over the world.

Humanity should heed the painful lessons that it has learned from the genocides of the 20th century and use that knowledge to build a world where peace with justice is established and memories are reconciled. In today's world, globalization challenges nations, religions and cultures to engage with one another in meaningful dialogue and creative interaction. We must move beyond interaction and dialogue to reconciliation by recognizing the truth and accepting each other. Negation and denial will not promote dialogue, restore justice, build peace or achieve reconciliation.

In the 20th century humanity paid dearly for a policy of silence in the face of genocide. It must not be silent in the 21st century. Here is the painful lesson that we carry with us. Here is also the great challenge before us.

10
LESSONS FROM THE GENOCIDE

1. INTRODUCTION

Following the genocide that took more than 1,000,000 human lives in 1994, many questions touching the church have been raised and still are being raised today. The period has been a time of finger-pointing and self-examination for the church in Rwanda. How could such tragedy occur in a country where the majority of the population is predominantly Christian? The census of 1991 showed that 88% of the Rwanda population were Christian, with 62% Catholics, 18% Protestant churches and 8% Adventists. Rwanda was considered as a success of evangelization in Africa, for Catholics as well as Protestants. While the Catholic Church could boast of a great success considering the number of adepts, the Protestant churches, particularly the Anglican church, could boast of the great East Africa revival that started from Gahini and spread like a wildfire through the neighbouring countries. How could genocide of the magnitude we all now understand happen in a country that was christianised to such a great extent? It is essential to understand some historical and social precedents to the genocide if we are going to draw lessons from what happened. The genocide did not fall on us like a clap of thunder from a blue sky; it was the culmination of a series of factors that started long before 1994.

Kigali: 10th anniversary memorial service to commemorate the genocide, April 2004.

2. SOCIAL/HISTORICAL CONTEXT

Rwanda is a small country of 26,338 square kilometres, with one of the densest populations of the African continent (approx. 8,500,000 people). From time immemorial, Rwanda has been populated by three ethnic groups: the Bahutu, the Batutsi and the Batwa. Calling them ethnic groups is a misnomer, as they all speak the same language without any dialects, have the same culture and live together in all the corners of the country. The history of the three groups prior to the genocide can be divided into three periods. Before the arrival of the colo-

BY ANTOINE RUTAYISIRE

nialists (up to 1900), the three groups lived together under the leadership of the same king. Not a single clash based on ethnicity is recorded during this period. But the power was in the hands of a monarchy with a Batutsi king surrounded by a nobility with a Batutsi majority. The Batwa were despised and segregated by the two other groups. The social situation was mobile, as a Muhutu who became rich could "kwihutura"; i.e., take off the Hutu identity and become a member of the Batutusi group.

Rwanda was first a German colony and then became a Belgian protectorate when Germany lost World War I. During this period, the ethnic configuration and sharing of power changed. Ethnic identity was put into identity papers and social mobility was no longer possible since the colonial administration preferred to educate the children of the Tutsi chiefs to the exclusion of the Bahutu and other people of the "lower" population.

3. THE COLONIAL PERIOD (1900-1960)

- All top administrative positions were reserved exclusively for the Batutsi who had been educated in the colonial schools;
- The divisive ideology of a superior race, of different geographical origins and chronological arrivals for the three ethnic groups was put into writing and taught;
- Forced labour, imprisonment, beating and heavy fines were imposed on the population by the colonial administration, but this was accomplished through the Batutsi leaders who later would come to bear the blame for all of that.

It is with this background that the period of independence dawned on Rwanda. To keep their power for a little longer, the colonial administration turned the population against one another based on those injustices enumerated above. The 1959 social revolution was an instance of the Bahutu turning against the Batutsi. This was the first ethnic clash in the history of the nation. Then began the successive Bahutu regimes that ruled until 1994.

Choirs are essential elements in the leadership of African worship.

4. THE REPUBLIC OR THE BAHUTU REGIMES (1959-1994)

Many people were killed during the revolution (1959-63), and many others left Rwanda to settle in neighbouring countries like Uganda, Tanzania, Burundi, Congo. The Batutsi refugees were refused peaceful return to the country for 30 years. Government policies based on ethnic discrimination were codified as laws and even incorporated into the national symbols (flag, anthem). Poverty and ignorance remained rampant in the population. Corruption, nepotism and regionalism increased with time and with them came a wave of discontent. The population increase was disproportionate to the growth of the economy, and that created dramatic pressure on land occupation. One political party exacerbated nepotism, regionalism and the general discontent. It was against this background that the Batutsi refugees attacked the country, organized as the Rwanda Patriotic Front, and this in turn sparked another wave of massacres against the Batutsi who had stayed inside the country, culminating in the genocide of 1994.

5. WHERE WAS THE CHURCH?

What can we learn from all this historical information? Where was the church when all of that was happening? The growth of Christianity in Rwanda came a bit late compared to some other countries on the continent: the first Catholic missionaries started their work in 1901. The expansion of the church was slow and difficult in the beginning but went faster when King Musinga, who was resistant to Christianity, was removed in 1930 and replaced by his son who had been educated in the colonial school of administration. The Protestant churches struggled under opposition from the Roman Catholic Church which was more influential with the colonial administration. In the 1930s, the Roman Catholic Church gained some momentum with greater acceleration in the 1940s when they baptized the new king whom they had helped ascend to power. This marked a milestone, when many people turned to Catholicism out of mere opportunism, a movement that came to be known as "the word of the king", Irivuze Umwam, or simply "toe the line of the leader". The Protestant churches also gained some momentum with the outbreak of the East Africa revival that spread from Gahini and reverberated within and far beyond the borders of the country. What did go wrong in this otherwise positive context?

The church from the very beginning, particularly the Catholic Church, has sided with the political regimes and has never raised a prophetic voice loud enough to challenge unjust systems. From the very beginning, the Protestant churches adopted a distant position, keeping away from what some missionaries called "worldly matters" like involvement in politics. The prophetic voice of the church was either silenced by close proximity to or too great a distance from the leaders. The end result is that the church has been either too close to the system and has shared its fate, or too distant and has become a bystander. The different injustices, the plight of the Batutsi refugees in the settlements, the different crimes committed against the Batutsi or against the members of the first republic, were all overlooked and never challenged. The church became an accomplice to the whole system of impunity that led to the genocide.

Looking at the kind of Christianity we were living during the period of the genocide and even before, it may be seen that nominalism was the fashion. As one missionary put it so well, "The country was sacramentalized but not christianized" Even those who were really converted were not discipled into responsible citizens so as to relate their faith to their daily lifestyles. Christianity was and is a religion rather than a way of belief and living. This led to a flawed theology. Most of the evangelical Christians lived with the mistaken idea that Christianity is a way to heaven not a roadmap to life in the world.

For example, I had never heard any teaching on the Bible and ethnicity until the period after 1990 when we started exploring together what had gone wrong. Even at that time, the analysis was shallow and timid because of the context. And the consequence was a deep wound inflicted on the human heart, mind and body. Destruction of infrastructures increased the level of poverty. Many educated people left Rwanda; others were killed or put

6. A Culture of Silence

7. Nominal Christianity

in jail. The return of the 1959-63 refugees increased the problem of land allocation. There were many orphans and widows with specific problems.

There remain problems of deep ethnic mistrust and trauma, and the prisons are full of people suspected of having taken part in the genocide. The challenge of rebuilding the country with this distressing legacy has forced us to engage in self-examination, and many important lessons have been learned as a result.

8. THE CHALLENGES FACING THE COUNTRY

The church seems to be more aware of its role in the process of healing the nation, and many endeavours are bearing fruit in that area. One can cite the prison ministries, different healing and reconciliation programmes, social reintegration for the former prisoners, as well as programmes with widows and orphans. All these have led to the rediscovery of the power of prayer in the process of healing the nation, and today the Rwanda prayer movement is growing strong; hence, there has been a rediscovery of the power of the message of the cross in healing and reconciliation. Although we can boast of some great achievements, we are still faced with many challenges that hinder the church in its impact on society, such as:

- Lack of unity among the leadership and the congregations. There is still a lot of competition and misunderstanding between the leaders, and this hinders the church's prophetic voice. A divided church cannot speak to a divided nation.
- Lack of a vision of what kind of society we want to build. Jesus was a builder of community, and the primitive church thought in terms of community. Acts 2-4 reflects this image of changed lives that build transformed communities.
- Lack of capacities – that is, lack of human and material resources to face up to the new situations. Our clergy are not trained well enough to compete with the cultural environment in shaping the new society, and the resources available are not enough to allow the church to face up to new situations.

Samuel Kobia with the prime minister Hon. Bernard Makuza of Rwanda.

If the church is going to regain its relevance for the future, it ought to take seriously the different challenges pointed out above and do the following:

- The church needs to rediscover its real identity as salt and light to the community. We need to shape a vision of the community we want to build under Christ's guidance and then act accordingly. It is only with a clear vision of the community we want to build that we will be empowered to do other things.
- We need to rediscover our unity as a body rather than live like competing political parties or rivals. Church leaders will start creating a different impression on the day when they rediscover each other as generals in the army of the same king, rather than captains of competing teams or generals of armies at war.
- We need to rediscover the biblical message that will help us shape the community on a biblical foundation. We need a different theology grounded in the life of the people without corrupting the message that has been given to us once for ever. We will become relevant on the day when we start scratching our communities and their members where they itch.
- We need to get nearer to the political leaders without having to identify with their ideologies; challenge them without hating them. We need to rediscover the art of speaking the truth out of love, and in love, for our communities and the leaders.
- We need to build the human capacities of our churches so that we shall have educated manpower able to shape and influence the communities.
- We need to rediscover our power found in prayer, the Word, total surrender to our Lord Jesus Christ and the guidance of the Holy Spirit.

9. CONCLUSION

RECLAIMING OUR DIGNITY

1. INTRODUCTION

The twentieth century was characterized by world wars, violent protests and revolutions. It was also witness to events which culminated in the genocide and massacre of millions of human beings. The main acts of genocide committed in the foregoing century targeted the Jews, the Armenians, the Cambodians and more recently the Tutsi in Rwanda. There are many similarities in most of these examples.

- Genocide anywhere was never perpetrated by coincidence but came as the result of fatal options. These options invariably have been conceived in arenas of power by a murderous state.
- Once conceived, plans for extermination have been meticulously prepared under the guidance of a totalitarian ideology whose end inevitably leads towards death.
- The victim is then diabolically transformed into a dangerous being. In effect, he or she is dehumanized.
- To justify their murderous policies, the perpetrators use slogans that are extremely persuasive and highly efficient.

The Hon. Edda Makabagwiza.

2. THE CASE OF RWANDA

BY HON. EDDA MUKABAGWIZA (MINISTER OF JUSTICE)

In Rwanda, the involvement of the population was most critical. The genocide perpetrated against Batutsi and the massacre of Hutus opposed to the ideology of division reached an extreme level of cruelty over a short period of about three months. As everywhere that genocide has been perpetrated, the Rwandan case invoked power politics during the period of the first two republics. The roots of the genocide can be traced to the period of colonial rule. Since 1959, various massacres similar to genocide were committed, yet the conspirators and perpetrators were never punished. This impunity continued for decades, and hence there was an anaesthetizing effect on the consciousness of sin in a section of the population. Political authorities were then blindfolded by hatred and gave themselves the right to dehumanize Tutsi who were no different from themselves. They enacted terrible atrocities on the people with the kind of treatment that would be unacceptable even in the case of animals.

Bishop Onesphore Rwaje welcomes ecumenical guests.

The genocide and massacres of 1994 have spoiled the image of the Rwandan people not only abroad but also in their own country. Genocide is undeniably a crime against humanity. It denies the first fundamental human right, which is the right to life. In the Rwandan memory, the country of a thousand hills has been conceived as a land full of milk and honey, where values such as friendship, brotherhood, solidarity, love, bravery and patriotism were the basis of social education and moral responsibility. National unity was made easier by the fact that Rwandan people have always shared the same history, culture and one common language. Beyond any prejudice, the people of Rwanda were known as hard workers, conscientious, honest and candid. Nevertheless, the genocide occurred in Rwanda. Yes, it happened, and it had its causes.

3. POLITICAL ORIENTATION

Power politics in Rwanda was one of the major causes of the genocide in 1994. We all remember the genocide as one of the ugly events of the 20th century because each of us was, in one corner or another, resident in the same world. In spite of early warning signs of the looming chaos, we were unable to prevent the tragedy. We had the obligation to protect victims, yet we failed to do so. This was a total failure on the part of all of us. The main cause of this failure was a lack of political goodwill. The situation questions the adequacy of our conscience as well as of our moral capacity to honour the human rights and dignity of our people.

4. JUSTICE AND GENOCIDE

Since the end of the 1994 genocide, Rwanda has made many efforts to face the question of justice, avoiding impunity as a means of refusing to deal with the crimes. History has taught us that the culture of impunity strengthens the roots of crimes against humanity. The Gacaca legal framework established since 2002 helps us to establish the space for fairness and justice. Moreover, this initiative contributes greatly to the recovery of the truth about genocide and affirms national reconciliation and the vision of a new unity.

5. CONSEQUENCES OF THE GENOCIDE

The 1994 genocide left with us numerous consequences. First there is our responsibility for reconstruction which is not only a tall order for Rwanda but also for the rest of Africa. The people of Rwanda have engaged in the effort of bringing about peace and security, putting in place institutions of good governance and orienting their politics towards unity and reconciliation in the nation. We believe that this orientation is a foundation of democracy, development and a total respect for human rights that have been violated for too long. We thank all those who have supported our efforts at reconstruction, though these remain insufficient in spite of the fact the government has allocated five percent of the budget to help victims and survivors of the genocide. The number of challenges is enormous given the fact that most of the survivors don't live in conditions of human dignity. Hence, we call upon the churches and people of good will for concrete support of our efforts because it is impossible to restore the full humanity to victims without creating the living conditions necessary for human dignity. Among vulnerable groups, we have women and girls who were victims of systematic rape used as a weapon during the genocide. Many of these women were infected by the HIV/AIDS virus. Infected women continue to die even today, so for them the genocide has not ended. We call upon all humanity to join hands with us in the immediate mobilization of resources and solidarity with the victims and survivors of the genocide in our beloved country.

6. RESPONSIBILITY OF PREVENTION

This is also a period of renewal and healing for us Rwandan people, and for all of those engaged in the struggle against the ideology of genocide. The culture of denial of the truth is the engine of a revisionist ideology in which some are taking refuge to avoid facing their participation or complicity in the genocide. We invite all partners to join the Rwandan people to condemn with all their energies any manifestation or campaign of revisionism vis-à-vis the 1994 genocide in Rwanda.

The wall has been breached, but what is now most important is to prevent at any cost any repetition of the genocide. The best way to do this is to accept and teach it as historical reality, bearing this tragic knowledge even if its weight is excessively heavy.

7. CONCLUSION

These reflections, and others that were shared before this event, are intended as an appeal to the international community for active solidarity in the prevention of genocide and its underlying ideology. We have a moral duty and goal to define strategies and networks throughout the world in order to raise consciousness within the international community that too often hesitates to commit itself because of the selfish interests of certain powers. The affirmation, "Never again", is to be translated into a firm commitment supported by a universally active solidarity.

RELIGION AND ETHNICITY

12

1. INTRODUCTION

While Africa is a continent with a strong and active religious life, my home country of Sweden is probably one of the most secularized countries in the world. At the time Christianity came to Rwanda, i.e. 100 years ago, Sweden had begun its transfer into a modern and secular society, where the role of the churches and the role of religion were marginalized for a period of time.

However, in both our contexts we can see an increased role of religion in politics. In the case of Sweden it can be described as a transfer from a post-Christian to a post-secular society. Unlike many European countries, Africa has the advantage and the disadvantage of meeting the challenges of trans-modern society, without the experience of processes of profound secularization.

Religion is normally not the source of conflict. However, depending on how religion is used or misused, religion can either de-escalate and help the conflict to be solved in a constructive way, or fuel the conflict, make it deeper, more violent and more difficult to solve. For the individual believer, religion is a single totality, but when reflecting on its political impact it can be helpful to explain the phenomenon of religion by classifying it according to its different forms of expression:

- Religion as spiritual experience. In this aspect there are only very slight differences between the world religions – Christianity, Judaism, Islam, Buddhism, Traditional and other religions.
- Religion as theology. In the past there were great differences between the major religions in this area, but in recent years they have moved towards a deeper common understanding.
- Religion as ethics and values. In this area there are much smaller differences between the religions than the individual believer and general public might think. For example, the three monotheistic religions have a similar basis for the

Peter Weiderud of the WCC with the Rev. Appoline Kabera.

BY PETER WEIDERUD

ethics of economic management and how to put one's gifts to good use – ideas about social justice, about the individual's responsibility for his or her neighbour and the global neighbourhood. In broad terms they all share the view that the earth can provide "enough for everyone's need but not for everyone's greed".

- Religion as a bearer of culture. This is the area where the greatest differences are to be found, not only between the world religions, but also within them. This aspect of religion is also increasingly important as the underlying causes of conflict – or as a tool easily manipulated in order to stir them up.

The two last-mentioned roles of religion, as an upholder of ethics and a bearer of culture, are aspects of religion that are not only the concern of individuals, the churches and religious organizations. I believe these aspects to be concerns for the whole society and that it is absolutely necessary to bring them into the decision-making and political processes of our societies. The fundamental transformations taking place in our societies mean that it is more urgent than ever to understand the role of religion in political processes. National change and global exchange have led to economic development of considerable magnitude. As millions of people leave extreme poverty behind, this potential offers hope to many of the world's poor. Old structures of power are forced to change.

Simultaneously, however, new patterns of exclusion and inequality have appeared, with marginalization, insecurity and powerlessness as real consequences for many people. Such a situation may generate feelings of social and cultural insecurity. Africa is the continent that is worst off in this respect.

These transformations in society also change the role of the nation-state. It would seem that the very rhythm and scale of the transformation exceed the capacity of national governments and policies to shape and influence the process. We have a global economy. But the legal, moral or democratic framework vital to an economy if it is to be able to serve the common good, continues to be a basically

2. RELIGION AND
FORCES OF MODERNITY

*Samuel and Ruth Kobia
enjoy an evening
of cultural presentations
in Rwanda.*

national responsibility. In the trans-modern, economic and political context, the main ideologies of the so-called modern 20th century – Marxism as well as liberal capitalism – have lost power as well as credibility. The nation-state as the main framework for identity, according to these ideologies, has become significantly weaker. Failed states are one of the most urgent security concerns in international affairs of today.

The nation-state is not going to disappear. It will remain the most important political instrument in the foreseeable future. But global interdependence makes it increasingly difficult for the nation-state alone to deliver what people expect for a good life. This is a fact in both the northern and the southern hemisphere.

Consequently, people will look for supplementary communities with which they can identify, both larger and smaller than the nation-state. But people will also turn inwards. Cultural factors – such as ethnicity and religion – will be more important in people's search for fundaments on which to build their hopes for the future. Socially and politically marginalized young people, who 30 years ago turned to Marxism in their search for a better future, might today turn to religion. Africa, with 2,600 ethnic groups and where colonial powers have injected mistrust and unrest for centuries, is particularly complex and challenging in this respect.

We know – both from history and contemporary experience – that religious influence on politics can be both beneficial and detrimental. Religious-political conflict is not a new phenomenon. Let me focus on three examples:

• Historically, the role of religion in political conflicts has been to increase tension – even cause clashes – between civilizations. This can happen only if religion is used by political leaders to emphasize the exclusiveness and primacy of one particular group at the expense of others – be it Christian, Jewish, Muslim or some other religious faith. It is necessary for all actors – in particular churches and ecumenical organizations – to counteract all such mono-cultural political tendencies and prove that the Samuel Huntington theory of an inevitable clash between civilizations is part of an outmoded way of thinking.

- In modern societies, in particular in confrontation with the modern ideologies of the 20 century, religious/political friction has mainly occurred between clerical and secular authorities. Basically this is a healthy conflict which has helped – and continues to support – the development of universal social values in modern society, for example, pluralism, democracy and human rights. It has also clarified the different role and relations between church and state.

- As a consequence of the transformation taking place in our societies, a third kind of religious/political clash has become more evident in recent years both in domestic and international politics. This is the split within religions and cultures. A split between "fundamentalists", who see their traditional scriptures and teachings as so absolute as to divide humankind into irreconcilable believers, and "infidels" and others, who see their ancient traditions or spiritual insights as raw material for wider human reconciliation, as the basis for an intensified search for community among people of differing races, creeds and national origins.

3. POWER POLITICS AND RELIGIOUS VALUES

The clash between cultural provincialism and openness is evident in all cultures and must be addressed with a forward-looking attitude. If religion is used as an instrument to gain political power and emphasize the exclusiveness and primacy of one's own group at the expense of others, it will be a most destructive contribution. The political idea of "the otherness" fuels conflicts. On the other hand,

- by emphasizing fundamental ethics and humanity,
- by giving voice to the voiceless,
- by emphasizing the responsibility of the individual,
- by focusing on inclusiveness and a deeper sense of hope,
- by highlighting the importance of the meeting of cultures,
- by being ecumenical,

religion will make a much needed and constructive contribution to our societies.

The WCC general secretary with the Hon. Abel Dushimimana.

In light of this, it is of growing importance for the ecumenical movement to work with member churches and to handle this split, to stimulate an inclusive understanding of the role of faith and to vaccinate against an exclusive understanding of themselves.

At the time of the Rwandan genocide I was serving as personal assistant to a bishop in the Church of Sweden and had very little connection to the WCC. I have talked to colleagues involved at that time, and they all say that we did not do enough in time. Since the tragedy, a lot of efforts have been made. However, when there still was time we failed to do enough. This is an in-built dilemma for a membership organization like the WCC. When member churches invite, encourage or give support, there is a potential for strong action, as with the US churches during the war on Iraq. As with South Africa in the struggle to end apartheid. As in Sudan during the struggle for a peace agreement.

However, when the churches are divided, when they oppose action from outside or when they are part of the problem, the space for action is very limited. This was the case in relation to communist countries in Central and Eastern Europe during the Cold War. This is the case with Zimbabwe today.

This dilemma needs to be further addressed. The more difficult the situation, the more important is the action and involvement from the ecumenical movement. The WCC and the ecumenical movement are not only accountable to member churches, but also to the people in these churches and to the principles of justice, peace and human rights that have been developed through our history. This is why criticism of the role of the WCC and the ecumenical movement before and during the genocide is important, not to blame, but to help to develop principles and criteria on how to act in situations when action is needed, when the local churches are not ready or not in consent with the action needed.

I would therefore like to hear comments on the role of the ecumenical movement in situations of great risk for major violations of human rights.

My experience tells me that it is particularly at the beginning of a conflict, or at the end, when the churches are mainly able to make constructive contributions. The closer we are to the peak of the conflict, the more difficult it is to find a relevant response.

The UN Charter gives governments and inter-governmental organizations clear measures of conflict prevention ("the Eliasson ladder"):
- early warning, verbal actions
- fact-finding by UN or regional organization
- stimulate parties to use different measures
- peace-keeping
- sanctions
- threat of force
- use of force, on the basis of chapter 7

4. THE INTERNATIONAL VALUE SYSTEM

5. CONCLUSION

The ecumenical movement could look for a similar structured approach to make the best possible use of our instruments – statements, pastoral visits, stimulating churches to act, fact-finding, dialogue with governments, advocacy campaigns, interaction with the UN etc.

Although it is clear that the WCC could have done more before and during the Rwandan genocide this does not mean that such actions could have prevented the genocide. A similar reflection is valid for the churches in Rwanda. To answer questions of what might have been, it is necessary to understand why genocide takes place. In literature and public debate, referring to the genocide of the 20th century – Armenian, Holocaust, Khmer Rouge and Rwanda – there are in particular three themes of explanations given. They relate to war, governance and ideology.
- Genocide takes place during war or in immediate connection with war. Preventing wars also means preventing genocide.
- They are carried out by non-democratic or semi-democratic regimes. Preventing genocide means long-term investment in democratic culture, including minority rights, legitimacy, independent judiciary, independent media etc.

- They are often based on exclusive ideologies, dividing us from them. Preventing genocide is about promoting tolerance.

All these themes are at the core of the ecumenical movement and the member churches. If we were to take them even more seriously, it would of course make a difference. Whether church action would have been enough to prevent the Rwandan genocide we cannot know. But it would have been enough to save many individuals and to avoid the painful question: Where were the churches during the genocide? This is our burden in history, to seek through memory renewal for the future, for the sake of generations to come.

Antoine Rutayisire chairs a plenary session of an ecumenical consultation on Africa.

13
THERE IS HOPE FOR AFRICA

1. INTRODUCTION

In solidarity with you we seek justice and forgiveness on behalf of God whose love draws all human beings to each other and fills the whole universe with tranquillity.

First and foremost I would like to share with you some basic insights into what I consider to be the historical location of the contemporary crisis of the human condition. We are faced today more than ever before with a crisis in human relations that is predicated on what I would describe as the melancholy of modernity.

The era of postmodernism has produced very advanced technologies and objects of wonder unknown in any period in history, but ironically has created conditions of estrangement that frustrate the human capacity to relate and value one another as human beings. The amazing capacity to transform things that God created into a new edifice does not necessarily correlate with the basic need for human beings to relate to each other as good neighbours. In the absence of social affection and capacity for social justice, even market values do not make sense. The greatest challenge to the church and the ecumenical movement is to provide safe spaces in which relationships can begin to flourish again and bear the fruits of peace for the rest of humanity.

Samuel Kobia addresses more than 800 participants.

2. THE MEMORY OF A VIOLENT CENTURY

On this very day we shall endeavour to transform the memories of genocide into an occasion of the rebirth of a new spirit full of equanimity that overflows to bring healing to the past and reinvent a new future with confidence and hope. Christians killed, and some were killed, Christians must speak about what really happened, confess and ask for forgiveness. We must ask constantly, where did we go wrong? Where were we as Christians when the atrocities were being planned and executed? What must we do to ensure that such events are never repeated again?

BY THE REV. DR SAMUEL KOBIA

The cries of vengeance will refuse to be silenced by history so long us we choose to allow our violent past to reclaim our consciousness of the future. When we think about the new rebirth of the spirit, let us never forget that memory is not just about a chronological record of social reality. By memory, in a theological sense, I am referring to the moral capacity to re-interpret events and organically relate them to the life of community. In memory we repent and seek to recover what has been lost, and gain what has been promised. Therefore we seek to learn from the events of history so that history does not have to repeat itself, because we can transform the trends of life and bring to light a new reality as a gift from God to the world. We therefore affirm the resolution to work together and to say once again with the people of Rwanda, "never again!"

We have just come to an end of the most violent century in the history of humankind, in which the proportion of human cruelty was unprecedented. Eric Hobsbawm, one of the most prominent historians of our time, says that the best estimate of "the century's mega-deaths is 187 million". He goes on to emphasize that "in the course of the 20th century, wars have been increasingly waged against the economy and infrastructure of states and against their civilian populations". Modern warfare and acts of genocide in the foregoing century targeted mostly poor populations and destroyed many critical sites of cultural and social memory of a people. The mutilation, not just in physical terms but in terms of psycho-social dimensions of being, is so vast that sometimes no language can capture the magnitude of human atrocities.

As the "century of massacres and wars" it has had great impact upon peoples' self understanding of their identities and the essential meaning of life; this impact will be measured only in generations to come. The mutilation of identities and maiming of memories have been part and parcel of the physical pain that many communities and societies had to endure with anguish. In the economy of war it is always the weak who die and the poor who pay the price. We live in a world whose fate seems to

3. VIOLENCE WITH IMPUNITY

remain in the hands of those blindfolded by the appetite for power in local and global spheres of life. Africa has had her share of contributing to the twentieth-century's 187 million deaths.

At the close of the century and in the early years of the 21st century Africa outdid every other continent in terms of brutality against civilians. And the 187 million deaths do not include the numbers contributed by the Rwanda genocide of 1994 because Hobsbawm's book was written before the atrocious event. The trend of molestation and abuse of children in the continent shows that we are losing the sacred regard for children as a gift from God. Chopping off babies' hands and gang raping two- and three-year-old girl children to death is the epitome of war against the very essence of what makes us human. It is not only un-African but also inhuman and anti-God to leave the African girl child helpless in the hands of rapists and murderers.

The systemic marginalization and discrimination based on gender relations and especially the rape of children as young as the tender age of even one year brings into question the social health of the African nations. Again, rape as a weapon of war is not just an issue which can be faced from legal retribution but must also be understood as part of spiritual warfare. In order to exorcize this ugly face of history, that constitutes our experience of the anguish of living, we must use the power of naming events as they truly occurred. Interpretation of events will always reflect the biases and prejudices of the times. However, today we can say that if the Rwanda event of genocide was the darkest moment in Africa in recent times, then the election of Mandela as the first truly democratically elected president of South Africa marked the highest sign of hope for a better Africa.

Those two diametrically opposed facts which took place in the same year, 1994, characterize the paradox of our continent at the close of the 20th century. The African paradox is characterized by a dual dilemma. It is the dilemma of a growing sense of optimism with clear evidence of positive historical progression, and yet at the same time there are sites of regression that suggest a pessimistic trend. Even though the influx of events may reflect a chaotic pat-

The Rev. Samuel Kobia of Kenya, general secretary of the World Council of Churches.

tern, nevertheless there is a continuum which signifies a gradual awakening of the continent. The spirit of optimism seems to override the clouds of uncertainty that often engulf the continent, yet one must acknowledge that peace has eluded Africa partly because of global intrusion into local politics.

In the nineties, after the end of the cold war and the crisis in Eastern Europe, there was a major wave of change in Africa which systematically led to new young leadership and created opportunities for democratic revolution also known as the second liberation. However, subsequent events in such countries as Côte d'Ivore, Liberia, Sierra Leone, Somalia and the Great Lakes Region began to undermine historical optimism for Africa. Yet even as the Lord's Resistance Army continues with its barbarous acts of senseless killings of innocent civilians and the pillage of the villages in Northern Uganda, the African Union has crafted a powerful and sharp vision of the New Partnership for Africa (NEPAD) which has truly become a beacon of hope for a new future for Africa. This initiative must obviously be anchored in the experience, values and aspirations of the people in the continent. Although a modicum of normalcy and peace has returned to some parts of Africa such as Sierra Leone and Liberia, where interfaith councils for peace and reconciliation have been working for several years now, there is still much to be done to establish a lasting foundation for peace in the continent.

4. THE WORK OF THE WCC

The diaconal work of the World Council of Churches has been advanced in solidarity with the liberation movements in Africa since the seventies and eighties, equipping the churches and social movements in solidarity with the poor and the oppressed while maintaining a critical distance from partisan engagement in power politics. New models of ecumenical solidarity have since then emerged, strengthening the capacities and renewing the institutional life of the ecumenical movement in Africa. We will begin a concerted effort in public education against violence and hatred in order to establish durable peace in our societies.

Schoolchildren consider the lessons of history.

The process of conscientization will lead to internal self-renewal of the church as a community of moral formation for peace. This must include initiatives for curriculum development of a catechism for peace to be used in the homes, in elementary as well as Sunday schools, secular schools and colleges, public bazaars and the palavers. Modelled on the WCC initiative of the Decade to Overcome Violence (DOV) and in particular the DOV document "Why Violence, Why not Peace?", this programme could provide a study guide to be translated into Kinyarwanda and other African languages. This booklet has had tremendous impact on the process of renewal and rebuilding confidence for lasting peace in wounded communities around the world and has been commended to the churches around the world.

The struggle to heal broken memories and traumatized psyches can happen not only in our quest for justice but also in rebuilding trust through confession and forgiveness. The consequences of the genocide in Rwanda are so deep that only through invoking the soul of the nation before God in utter yearning for healing can we overcome the cruelty of the past. What happened in Rwanda reminds us of how ancient rivalries are transformed through colonial memory into the flames of violence that could not be extinguished, even by the moral claims of the church.

As the continent and her peoples are constantly under cultural siege and perpetually being mutilated by internal and external forces of conquest we must remember that our hope is embedded in vigilance with the Word of God which speaks to us in the spirits of our ancestors, and ultimately is revealed in the exemplary life and value of the Jesus narrative.

It is by standing in solidarity with the suffering, and because of Rwanda's determination to live beyond the past and celebrate the resurrection, that the ecumenical movement can contribute to optimism for a new life for the people of Rwanda. Jesus is for us the embodiment of a living narrative of hope in Africa.

The capacity for survival and the revival of the inner spirit beyond the features of an oppressing world have been exemplified in the singing traditions of the African people, especially in the case of South Africa during apartheid. They sang away their oppression to the amazement of those who tortured and treated them with great indignity. A people who lived their history as if it was no longer their own, did not seek retribution as the basis for correcting that history. In this regard the churches together created the moral space in which all the forces of liberation in South Africa found a home and a place for ecumenical bonding. It is in the quality of Christian life and not in the claims we make that the church becomes truly a moral community whose boundaries of identity are not restricted by articulation of dogmatic formulations of faith. The stories of survival invoke memories and pose a dilemma about the ambivalence of the claims we make for the church. Religious impulses, especially those of puritan origin, tend to privilege dominant identities in the global naming systems. The question of identity, in the naming of the other as inferior and as an object of subjugation, creates grievances that have deep and major consequences for public security.

The matrix of identity contains social material that camouflages the inner power of naming and being named. The use of human morphology – physical appearances and complexion to classify people and create a hierarchy of power relations between "tribes" is part and parcel of the lie of racism. The rhetoric of privileged identity and the claims of a civilizing mandate create a very unhealthy environment in which violence comes to be justified even as having an ontological value. As is often the case, those who are subjects of conquest become victims of their own history unless they change it and reclaim it from the oppressing powers of this world.

The suffering and misery experienced in Africa today is an invitation to the vocation of restoration of human dignity. It is further an invitation to awaken the hearts and minds of Africa's own people, the authentic hope of a new life of abundance and fulfillment. But until and unless the question of the

5. THE CHURCH AS A MORAL COMMUNITY

dignity of every individual person is affirmed, respected and upheld, democratic experiments in Africa will remain hobbled and futile, without focus. We cannot speak of the church as the moral community if we do not experience dignity in the church and if she does not facilitate the value of human dignity. The church ought to be informed and nourished by the ethical value systems anchored in the African worldview.

In the modern capitalist economy, to be is to have money and to become is to consume. From the African traditional worldview the individuality of a person, as created by God, is all that matters and cannot be substituted or valued for relations with others. The person's dignity and worth is not, therefore, incumbent upon one's monetary wealth. To be is to be in relationship with other human persons and with the creator. But the question of dignity is not exclusive to the realm of human experiences; it includes especially institutions that also mediate those experiences. Part of the process of restoration of dignity is reconstruction of the legitimacy of our own institutions and reclamation of the kind of leadership that is a prerequisite to lasting peace.

Samuel Kobia greets the president of the Presbyterian Church in Rwanda.

The Rwandan genocide is forcing us to confront one basic truth of human dignity. We cannot trivialize the unacceptable; we must trace the chain of the events that led to genocide in Rwanda. We cannot allow ourselves to be abandoned by history. As human beings we cannot assume that the kind of conflicts that go out of control are isolated from the ecology and economy of life. As one writer once said, "nothing is to be feared, only understood", thus, we must unravel the matrix of social relations and initiate a process of comprehending the undergirdings of genocide. We should never shy away from our bloody past. The complicity of the church in the events of the Rwandan genocide are common in other historical moments and experiences elsewhere in the world. However, we can remember that Dietrich Bonhoeffer and many persons of heroic faith have acted with prophetic courage in the midst of human atrocities. It is this courage that eventually produces the church as the new peaceable moral community.

6. THE POWER OF MEMORY

Good memories are the social landscape of the spirit that guides our dreaming of the world with abundant possibilities for life. Without the spirit there is no memory and without memory there would be no dreams that keep the world alive. And therefore there would be no hermeneutic to connect the present with the past as we move towards a new future. Our active capacity to remember sets the powers of memory to work against future evils. There is the obvious past, there is the remembered past, there is the recorded past. The past is very large, and it gets larger every minute: we do not know all of it (Lukacs John, *At the End of an Age*, Yale University Press, New Haven, 2002, p.52). As time recedes, the events of the past are coloured with ambiguity as if they are no longer the fabric and essence of a moral present in the case of genocidal memory. Indeed time advances inside us more as a flood moves through space. Behind the water is more water, which is why the water moves. Only the water of memory can reveal to us the secrets of time (this is a translation of the Portuguese poet, José Saramago, 1988 Nobel Laureate, expressing the elasticity of memory).

The water of memory as a symbol is deep and most profound; none can fathom her depths because history is a multitude of events like the waves in the high seas. But what happens to memory when there is no historical record? We forget! And what happens if there is nothing to remember? And what if that which is to be remembered is defined by our inhumanity as in the case of genocide?

The thing outside the possibility of memory is the spirit. Nothing precedes the spirit for it lingers on even in the void of history where memory cannot be verbalized. Hence we must be anchored in the kindred spirit, in other words it is the Holy Spirit that replenishes the good things in history and relieves us of the burden of the past! The effects of trauma and the injuries of institutional evils would be healed not just by the passage of time but rather by coming face to face with the realities that have made Africa what it is today. May we have reached the time when all the children of Rwanda look beyond the memories of affliction that led their

A survivor of the Rwandan genocide tells of his experience.

parents and guardians to be scattered by the sword of death into the foreign lands of endless toil! And may they all come back home and find solace and peace in rebuilding this great nation! Yes, may this be the time when those who went away because of the violence and anguish of human finitude come back to console others again, and remind them that they are part of Africa, the womb of life, and as part of Africa they are the bosom of all creation. With confidence we at the World Council of Churches embrace the people of Rwanda and will walk with them hand in hand to rebuild the future as we pave the way for the new dawn of the kingdom of God upon the people of Africa.

7. Conclusion

In conclusion, I wish to identify the key issues and inquiries that would make for durable peace in Africa:

- We need to come to terms with our history as Africans and make an honest assessment of the benefits of hindsight so that we are better placed to address the root causes of events such as civil wars and even genocide.
- We need to know how to manage memory and to be emancipated from painful memories into a new rebirth of the kindred spirit so that we may re-invent the future with confidence and hope.
- In this regard we strongly affirm the human dignity of all, based on African heritage and the sanctity of life.
- We need to develop new skills on how to interpret identity: the 21st century will be dominated by the politics of naming otherness, hence the need to comprehend ethnic/tribal identities as resources of diversity rather than differences to be condemned.
- It is vital that we re-interpret the memories of boundaries and comprehend the notion of territoriality.
- The churches ought to accompany and affirm good leadership and good governance in Africa: there is need to verify the causes of conflicts and develop alternative frameworks of engaging civil society and state institutions in Africa.

14
THE CHURCH AND UNITY IN AFRICA

1. INTRODUCTION

To the beloved people of Rwanda: I bring greetings from the African Church and I hereby assure you of our commitment to justice and forgiveness. We pray that this will be a point of renewed and concerted effort by the church to help foster healing and transformation for the whole continent of Africa!

In this struggle with the memory of genocide we add our view to the church's collective repentance and renewed search for the face of God who is ultimately the source of healing and perfect unity in diversity. Even in the midst of contradictions inherent in the multiplicity of identities like religious, denominational, ethnic and racial identity, we know that we have to strive to embrace that which brings us together to celebrate our differences with dignity. The suffering and struggles born out of the negative history of genocide in Rwanda should not make us hostage to the reality of anguish forever; neither should we surrender to the global and local forces of tyranny. Rather let us be faithful to the claim that our God is the One in whom history becomes consummated and fulfilled.

The Rev. Dr Mvume Dandala speaks with conviction in Kigali.

It is this truth that we need to find a way to restore to the centre of the journey of the people of Rwanda. If it is difficult for the Rwandan people to embrace it, it would be understandable, but we must never give up trying. For this is the only hope we have to overcome the consequences of human sin that give birth to tragedies such as we have encountered. The struggle to heal wounded memories and our traumatized spirits happen not just in our quest for justice but also in rebuilding trust through confession, forgiveness and honest reflection on the entire history that gave rise to this tragedy. Only then shall we celebrate together with the rest of creation the harmony that is promised and the peace that is given beyond the conflicts of this world.

BY THE REV. DR
H. MVUME DANDALA

The consequences of the genocide in Rwanda are so deeply perplexing that only through invoking the soul of the nation before God in utter yearning for healing and unity can we overcome the cruelty of the past. What happened in Rwanda could have happened elsewhere given the conditions in Africa of ancient rivalries that were trapped and manipulated by colonial memory. The call of the church is to be in solidarity with the people of Rwanda in their suffering and quest for nationhood. The church must find a way to help the Rwandans to live beyond the past and celebrate the resurrection of a new future for Rwanda. That is how Jesus becomes for us the living hope for Rwanda and Africa. I therefore invite this great nation with the accompaniment of the All Africa Conference of Churches to become the beacon of hope for the rest of Africa. Show us that from the ashes of death a new dawn of hope and abundant life can welcome the whole continent in unity and peace.

2. THE COMMUNITY OF MEMORY

When we become church, we celebrate memory. Memory of the one in whom we are offered new life and are united to the mystery of the Triune God. Before Jesus left this world, he said to his disciples "do this in memory of me". He makes us to be one and unites us as friends, as a people, as a church, because he has promised that he is always with us. Ours is to make the community of the Church a community of memory. It is the space of memory that produces a sensitive, caring, healthy and morally vigilant community.

In the presence of God the church is called to be a community of unity in spite of our diversity. Hence our responsibility and our obligations to reclaim the original gift of the unity of humankind to serve in the presence of God. Disunity and mistrust in the human family began with disobedience against God and consequently became a crime against humanity and the entire creation. The crime of Cain is epitomized by the sarcastic response to the compassionate appeal by God, "where is your brother?", when he says "am I my brothers keeper?". This crime reminds us of the arrogance of humanity in the face of our need to care for each

Joy and hope are alive in the worship of the churches.

other as children of one God. We are here today to remember those to whom we were called to be keepers, yes, those who have been mutilated by the negative forces of human history; and to strengthen the quest for all to be keeper to each other.

The moral claims of authority by the church form the basis by which the church becomes not only the conscience of society but also the caring, unifying, prophetic community. It is true that many church leaders are doing monumental work to prevent a repetition of what happened to the people of Rwanda. We affirm and acknowledge their effort and commit ourselves to accompany them in the search for the healing of their land and lasting unity in our mother continent. The church in Rwanda has humbly confessed its inadequate response to the genocide. We all join them in this confession. It has confessed that it may have participated directly or indirectly in the perpetuation of this tragedy, in the true tradition of discipleship it has sought forgiveness and re-empowerment in order to become a healing agent. In this regard it is correct for the ecumenical movement in Africa to confess its own paralysis that reduced it to the role of a bystander in the event of the genocide.

And so we are in solidarity, Rwanda, not as part of a standing international presence but as part and parcel of the experience of pain, guilt and anguish so that we may walk together in a process of healing of memories. Never again should the churches in Africa watch helplessly when any part of this continent is engulfed in senseless destruction. Our confession on this altar of Rwandan sacrifice as a church in Africa is also our public committal never to allow ourselves to be reduced to complacent, indifferent and paralyzed bystanders to any tragedy!

We must therefore be awakened to act with a sense of urgency in order to pre-empt and prevent such events ever occurring again in any part of Africa. The way in which the church in Africa handles this problem will show whether it has passed the test of maturity. The fight against ethnic discrimination is an important prerequisite for an effective evangelism. No great help from outside, from whichever organization, can sow the spirit of love and forgiveness among the Tutsi and Hutu in Rwanda, and no great financial aid or external involvement can create peace in Africa, so long as there is neither the atmosphere nor the environment in which we can find one another beyond ethnic differences in order to embrace and celebrate each other as African children of God. Our evangelization must help us find one another in this way. We have to explore the task and call for evangelization that enhances responsible nationhood.

The ecumenical movement in Africa must provide the space in which the negative forces of ethnicity are expunged and give way to positive, dignified identities of nationhood that will flourish towards celebrated, dignified African consciousness. The movement for emancipation of the negative identity of the African people was initially expressed in the works of African poets and philosophers such as Aimé Césaire, Frantz Fanon, Amilcar Cabral and Léopold Sédar Senghor. The concept of "negritude" – a return to the cultural traditions of the black people as well as the demand for the abolition of colonialism, was coined by Aimé Césaire in the early nineteen thirties. At the heart of negritude is the uniqueness and strength of what it means to be human and African contrary to the vestiges of western individualism and ethnicism. To this, we add the need to be an authentic African Christian. The negritude movement provides a great challenge and opportunity for ecumenical renewal as an ongoing process that calls for discernment and action for peace and stability in Africa.

Our commitment to a new sustainable future must therefore be anchored in common values of proclaiming the good news beyond the realms and limits of social, political and class discourse. The centrality and meaning in proclaiming anew the promise of the new future ought to reflect our capacity to be good neighbours. The ecumenical movement in Africa ought to provide the space of neighbourhood in which the relationships between peoples and institutions are guided by the moral traditions of abundant life. Every activity in our institutions must remain structured around solidarity with the weak and the excluded in society. This is

3. THE CHURCH BEYOND ETHNIC BELONGING

The proclamation of hope beyond the harsh realities of history.

the gospel of Jesus Christ as it should be proclaimed to give abundant life to Africa.

Today our common challenge in the ecumenical movement in Africa is to develop alternative models, indicators and early warning systems that will give us a comprehensive understanding of the prevailing conditions that may lead to genocide in any part of Africa. While poverty and disease are on the increase in most parts of the continent, the struggles for the well-being of the poor and the weak must remain on top of our agenda together. If need be, we must re-think institutional forms of ecumenism and church formation, especially if these inhibit or cease to express the aspirations for unity among ordinary Christians beyond conflictual ethnic identities. We have to focus on the tendency of the church to be ethnic-based in its formation. In many African contexts this is true. Only a determined ecumenical initiative will help us to manage and remove this potentially destructive sting of Christian mission.

The spirit of unity lives and dwells among ordinary people in the villages and communities across Rwanda and the entire continent. There are so many Africans of diverse ethnic identities living side by side. The African heritage in many ways enables us to craft alternative ways of dialogue and learn to live with diversity, because there is in our culture the intrinsic structure of tolerance. It is therefore essential that the Christian faith revitalize such capacities as exist within African traditional belief systems.

4. CONCLUSION

The way the genocide in Rwanda has been perceived and named also reflects the ideological categories of identities as they are constructed by global powers. The popular notions of tribalized identities tend to oversimplify the nature of the genocide in Rwanda and elsewhere. Hence it is essential that the alleged complicity of certain countries in the northern hemisphere in the instigation of the genocide in Rwanda should be subjected to public inquiry. We must, as the All Africa Conference of Churches and the World Council of Churches, help develop initiatives in which the process of healing and reconciliation in Rwanda will extend to such countries. Given the fact that the conflicts in Africa are connected to, and sometimes are produced by, global interests, it is imperative that the ecumenical movement activate the church worldwide to counter these foreign forces of destruction in Africa.

Whichever framework one uses to name the phenomenon of genocide it should never explain away the moral burden of the people themselves and their moral institutions to prevent genocide. The effects of trauma and the injuries derived from institutional evils would be healed not just by the passage of time but rather by coming face to face with the realities that have made Africa what it is today. We affirm the commitment of the people of Rwanda to their healing processes of Truth and Reconciliation, namely Gacaca. We acknowledge the magnitude of this task, but having committed to the process we salute the Rwandan people for their determination to ensure that its outcome leads to reconciliation rather than vengeance. The ecumenical movement must do all in its power to ensure that the experience of reconciliation in Rwanda becomes a model for other nations in the continent for the restoration of the dignity of all Africans.

In the life story of Jesus we encounter the nexus of unity for all beings and creation in the awesome presence of unconditional giving of the self to God. We locate our search for unity as an act of reciprocity to the unity that already exists within the Triune God. We are part of the larger movement of the Holy Spirit seeking to bring humankind and the whole creation into communion with one another and with God.

Our resolve therefore is never to let go the hand of God. May God bless the people of Rwanda, May God Bless Africa, guide her leaders, guard her children and give Africa peace!

15

TOWARDS JUSTICE AND NON-VIOLENCE

1. INTRODUCTION

The impressive and solemn gathering at Kigali stadium.

BY HIS HOLINESS ARAM I

I regret not being with you today. I can assure you that my prayers and thoughts will be with you this afternoon. As we come together in this stadium let us say together "glory be to God", because He has brought us together as one people of God. Let us say together, "glory be to God", because there is hope for Africa. "Glory is to God" because in the power of His Spirit Africa is committed to lasting peace. As Christians we believe that there can be no lasting peace without justice. Furthermore, we believe that working for peace means doing justice; and doing justice in Africa means being with the poor and against all those who make people poor. Doing justice in Africa means being with those affected by the AIDS epidemic; doing justice in Africa means promoting democratic values and ensuring people's participation in decision-making, doing justice in Africa implies doing justice for Africa by strengthening the special place and unique role of Africa in the international communi-ty. Rwanda is, geographically speaking; a small country with a tiny population at the heart of the African continent, but it is a country whose richness resides in its spiritual and moral values, in its com-mitment to peace with justice, to human dignity and human rights. I am so happy to be with you at this important moment in your history, and to share your memory and experience, your hope and vision.

I come here as the Moderator of the World Council of Churches. The WCC is a global fellow-ship of churches, and the churches of Rwanda are members of this organization. Issues related to peace, justice and human rights are at the heart of the vocation of the WCC. I come here, also, as the Head of a Church whose members were the victims of genocide at the beginning of the 20th century. In fact, the Armenian genocide was the first genocide of the 20th century, and the genocide in Rwanda the last genocide of the 20th century. Therefore, our two nations have gone through the same experience; and today we stand together and demand justice and accountability from the international community.

As I stand before you, I want to tell you that after so many years of silence, the Armenian genocide was mentioned for the first time early in the 1980s in the United Nations, and the person who mentioned the Armenian genocide in his report to the Human Rights Commission of the United Nations was one of your distinguished sons from Kigali, Professor Nicodem Ruhashyankiko. He was appointed as special rapporteur in 1971, at the 24th session of the Human Rights Commission of the United Nations, to prepare the report on the Convention of 1948 and the Armenian Genocide. Therefore, I would like to seize this opportunity to express on behalf of our people our gratitude to you. I would like also to express our full support to you in your commitment to strengthen your internal unity and achieve reconciliation together, after your painful experience of genocide some ten years ago. I want on this occasion to emphasize four points:

- Christianity is a religion of non-violence.
  The Christian religion is, indeed, a religion of non-violence. Our Lord Jesus Christ told us to reject violence. Therefore, as Christians we are called to overcome violence by non-violence; to conquer evil by good. To say "no" to violence in all its forms and expressions is not a passive attitude; it is a courageous act and a responsible decision to go through suffering for those values and truths that are brought to the world as gifts of God by Jesus Christ.

Today the church is central to the hope for a new Africa.

- Christianity is a religion of peace. Peace is a God-given gift. Through His incarnation our Lord Jesus enriched the life of human beings with peace. Peace is also a divine mission entrusted to all Christians. Working for peace is an essential dimension of our Christian life and witness; it is integral to being Christian: therefore peace-building must become a clear priority for Christians in the midst of violence, hatred and conflicts.

- Christianity is a religion of justice. Justice is at the heart of Christian faith and mission. One cannot understand the gospel of Christ without justice. In fact, our Lord not only prayed for justice but He worked for it; He shed his blood for justice. Being Christian also means struggling for justice; being Christian means rejecting and challenging all those structures which generate and perpetuate injustice.
- Christianity is a religion of reconciliation. Reconciliation means living together, working together and struggling together on the basis of common values and in spite of our differences and particularities. Reconciliation must be based on truth, mutual respect and acceptance. Christianity does not believe in cheap reconciliation. Any real reconciliation must be based on confessing the truth and committing ourselves to justice and peace. This is the true way leading us to reconciliation.

The commemoration of the 10th anniversary of the genocide in Rwanda is an occasion for you to remember those victims: your sisters and brothers, your parents, your sons, your pastors, your community leaders and all those who lost their lives during one of the most tragic periods of your history. We must not forget our martyrs. The martyrs are the living source of our spiritual strength, our hope and vision. This is also an occasion for you to demand justice and accountability. All those who organized or supported the genocide must be accountable. And all those who suffered, reparation must be made for all those who suffered. This is also an occasion for you to look forward by engaging yourselves in the process of reconciliation and nation-building. Let us say together "plus jamais la violence". Let us together commit ourselves to justice with peace in Rwanda and in all Africa. Glory be to God. God bless you all.

16
THE KIGALI COVENANT

Love your neighbour as yourself. Mark 12:31

This covenant with God and with each other is based on the second most important commandment ever given to humanity, found in Mark 12:31.

We, Christians, from the churches in Africa and beyond, thank God for making it possible for us to gather at the workshop on Lasting Peace in Africa, in Kigali, Rwanda, from 14 to 19 April, 2004.

We came to Kigali to stand in solidarity with the people of Rwanda who suffered terribly the horror of genocide that claimed the lives of more than one million innocent people in 1994. We listened to the testimonies of the survivors of the genocide, and visited genocide remembrance sites where we saw with our own eyes evidence of people's inhumanity to people. As some Rwandan churches have already done, we accept before God guilt for inaction during the genocide in Rwanda and offer our apology to the people of Rwanda.

Public reading of the Kigali Covenant, and a call to a just peace and reconciliation.

We saw the remnants of the genocide in the form of bones, skulls and dilapidated clothing and personal belongings of babies, children, youth and adults. They were frighteningly displayed, as reminders of the dark hundred days that the Rwandan genocide lasted, at the Ntarama Memorial (formerly a Roman Catholic chapel) as well as at the Kigali Memorial Centre. We also heard stories of women of the genocide who were raped and who are today living with HIV/AIDS and bruised bodies, of households now headed by children and of totally handicapped persons. These the ecumenical family must undertake to assist in any way possible.

DATED THIS 18TH DAY OF APRIL 2004 IN KIGALI, REPUBLIC OF RWANDA.

As we pondered the stories of genocide, we were convinced that the perpetrators of the genocide had destroyed their own humanness, cut off their relationship with God, before they could take away the humanness of others. The depth of the horror challenged us to reflect deeply on strategies and means by which we can build everlasting peace in Rwanda in particular, and the rest of Africa in general.

The abuse, anger, tension, humiliation, trauma, pain and tears inherent in any genocide experience like that of Rwanda remind us of the events leading to the crucifixion of our Lord Jesus Christ (Matt. 27).

The false accusations and torture of the innocent are truly degrading, to say the least, and an affront to the gospel of Christ. Hence, like Peter the apostle, the best human response would have been to encourage the victims to draw their swords in revenge; and yet Jesus ordered Peter, his disciple, to put back his sword. Christ, the Master, warns that those who kill by the sword will die by the sword (Matt. 26:48-52).

The Kigali Covenant was read to the assembled crowd in three languages.

This is an experience that teaches us to struggle for peace at all costs. This is why as Christians we teach and preach confession and repentance before the message of peace, reconciliation and love to all and sundry. We thank God for the victory of Easter – for bringing us back to life, for bringing Rwanda, back to life. The significance of Easter is that Christ rose victorious over death.

We are therefore grateful to God, the Sustainer and Giver of Life, for the hope and courage found within and among Rwandans who embarked with determination on the process of reconstruction of this beautiful country, leading to reconciliation among its sons and daughters.

Many countries on our continent have the potential of repeating the Rwandan experience, and now that we have time to prevent a similar occurrence, we commit ourselves that never again shall such a degree of violence and crime against humanity be allowed to occur in any of our countries. Consequently, we in the workshop have dwelt on identifying issues such as manipulation of ethnic identities and dominant tribal attitudes that have the potential to destabilize the continent of Africa, and we do hereby covenant with God and each other to:
- Share widely our experience and invite all persons of good will to work for peace in Africa and the world at large.

- Work and promote good governance practices that protect the integrity and dignity of creation.
- Stand up and speak against behaviour, pronouncements and practices that have the tendency to set one group of people against another.
- Challenge the youth and the leadership of churches and governments to feed the minds and souls of their people with love, peace and reconciliatory messages so that painful experiences in human memory are not exploited.
- Pledge to ensure that never again should Africa experience genocide.
- Pledge with the World Council of Churches, the All Africa Conference of Churches, the Sub-Regional Fellowships, National Christian Councils and all other confessional and religious bodies to help build the capacity of our churches in advocacy and be proactive in the prevention of conflicts.
- Regularly call on organizations such as the African Union and the Regional Economic Blocs to ensure that rapid-response mechanisms are in place to prevent wars and acts of genocide.

We were touched and overwhelmed by reports on the efforts of the Rwandan government, churches and humanitarian agencies promoting solidarity and acts of healing among the victims of the genocide, although more resources are needed to complete the task of restoration.

We therefore call for a strong advocacy effort and support of the healing process currently taking place in Rwanda. While we plead for support for the efforts of the Rwandan government, the churches are encouraged to bear witness through prophetic ministry by standing for truth, justice and reconciliation.

As we renew our covenant with God and each other, we assure all genocide victims across the globe that you are in our hearts as we seek to fulfill these promises. We invite men and women of goodwill to accompany us in this journey aimed at the restoration of the integrity of humanity in our troubled world.

VOTE OF THANKS

The Hon. Charles Murigande.

By the Hon. Charles Murigande (Minister of Foreign Affairs and Co-operation)

On behalf of the government and people of Rwanda I wish to thank all the distinguished church leaders from the World Council of Churches, the All Africa Conference of Churches and from various countries in the continent. We hereby express our profound gratitude to all those who have endeavoured to make this opportunity a reality. We are not only grateful for the awesome presence of the churches together with the people of Rwanda in this occasion of remembrance but also for showing solidarity with us in facing and dealing with our challenges of the past and present.

Indeed, what happened in Rwanda was a tragedy, and in the name of the Rwandan government and the people of Rwanda, I affirm that your presence and especially your message is a great comfort to us. We have received encouragement on different occasions from the work that you do and the moral courage entailed in your mission. All this invigorates the hope for healing of memories among the people of Rwanda. We are very grateful that you not only have accepted our invitation but also extended the same invitation to other leaders of the churches in Africa. The Kigali Covenant is a declaration before God of your own commitment vis-à-vis the Rwandan people. This covenant carries an important, threefold message of hope and gratitude.

- First and foremost, it is an expression of the gratitude of the people of Rwanda for your untiring commitment to fight all forms of genocidal ideologies that are rampant nowadays, especially in our sub-region, through the radio and newspapers.
- The covenant is also an expression of your commitment to talk about what you have seen which is often denied by the perpetrators and those who are not directly concerned. The act of genocide is a flagrant crime against humanity and therefore bears a heavy responsibility. The denial of

genocide is common even in today's world. It is for this reason that the Armenians are still struggling with their history so that the world may recognize that they are victims of denial. The Government of Turkey continuously tries to deny this fact and this proves to us that genocide is a terrible crime for which no one wants to bear responsibility. While the international community has recognized the genocide against Jews, some people still deny it, and this is the same in the case of Rwanda. Your role in testifying about what you have heard and seen is critical indeed as part of the process in bringing about truth and justice in Rwanda.

• As you have expressed in the Kigali Covenant, we must never forget the victims of these crimes against humanity, lest we allow ourselves to be surprised by another tragedy of such magnitude. The survivors live under unacceptable conditions such as being homeless and traumatized, but this is an invitation for the mobilization of resources in response to their need. I have no doubt that the churches together have the capacity to take action and enable us to face this overwhelming task.

Again, on behalf of the government and the people of Rwanda: we applaud the continued support and accompaniment of the World Council of Churches and the All Africa Conference of Churches. While many may not be aware of your actions, you have been a great blessing to us. And we hope that, through our tears, you will be blessed.

Dedicated to the memory of

Patriarch Petros VII demonstrated a pastoral love for Africa and all its people.

Pope Petros VII, Patriarch of Alexandria and All Africa (1949-2004)

"…God is the one who gives us strength to live in unity and mutual understanding which we particularly need in these times of fear and disaster.

"We give praise to God and ask him to grant peace, love, equality and solidarity to people of different races and to those practising different religions so that we can see the peace of God reign in the hearts of us all.

"We seek a society that consists of people of different races, colours, descent and language living in brotherly love…"

PATRIARCH PETROS VII
DAY OF PRAYER FOR PEACE IN THE WORLD
ASSISI, ITALY, JANUARY 2002

An early promoter of the ecumenical movement, Dr Beyers Naudé became an active opponent of apartheid in church and state.

and

Dr Beyers Naudé, former general secretary of the South African Council of Churches (1915-2004)

"…his life is a shining beacon to all South Africans − both black and white. It demonstrates what it means to rise above race, to be a true South African. If someone asks me what kind of person a New South African should be, I will say: take a look at Beyers and his wife Ilse."

PRESIDENT NELSON MANDELA
SPEECH ON THE OCCASION
OF BEYERS NAUDÉ'S 80TH BIRTHDAY,
CAPE TOWN, SOUTH AFRICA, MAY 1995

FOR A NEW
AFRICA
With Hope and Dignity

95

Printed in France by SADAG
September 2004